Praise for
Reta

"This book is a welcome te
is direct, practical and inc
will find this book most h
blueprint for retailers. Th
the best practice for retail
students, aspiring retailer
to improve."

TAN WEE 1

"This book is a valuable re
more about the exciting v
the fundamental issues c
step-by-step approach m
read for both students an

Instit

"*Retail Operations: How to*
practical guide written ir
of key areas of retail that
be used as a quick refere
retail industry. The book
the retail industry."

Aussino Group Ltd

"Our company is honoured to have had invited both Angie and Sarah as our trainers. Their trainings had increased our knowledge on retail management, and inspired our retailers to put in efforts to improve the management of their stores, which helped in our endeavour to grow as professional sports retailers.

On the whole, the book acts as a very practical tool. Its analytical approach, together with its precise explanation, practical guidelines and realistic experiences, made the book suitable to both the experienced retailers who may find solutions to their retail problems from the book and to the new entrants who find the book educational."

IRIS FANG, *Visual Merchandising Manager,*
Nike Sports (China) Co., Ltd

"Retailing is one of the oldest trades. Today, retailing is a sunrise industry. With consumers being the main focus of all business activities, the retailing function has taken on a new dimension. Almost everyone is talking about satisfying consumers' needs and wants. New retailers are mushrooming. Existing retailers are facing new challenges.

I congratulate Angie and Sarah for successfully presenting in this new edition insightful thinking and realistic ideas that leave the readers with a better understanding of modern retailing."

WONG KAI HONG, *President,*
Retail Professional Network

RETAIL OPERATIONS

SECOND EDITION

"This book by Angie Tang and Sarah Lim is highly readable and commended. It comprehensively covered almost all that one needs to know to run one's own store. It is a very good working guide for new entrants to the retail business. Even experienced retailers and shopping mall managers can gain some useful insights reading it."

TONG KOK WING, General Manager,
Investment Properties, Frasers Centrepoint Limited

"Retailing has become one of the fastest growing segments of the economy as many new entrepreneurs enter the retail business for the first time. Unfortunately most have no one to turn to for professional advice and they usually learn how to set up their business the slow, hard and oftentimes expensive way – through trial and error.

The second edition of *Retail Operations: How to Run Your Own Store*, provides new retailers with practical advice on how to successfully plan, launch and manage their own stores effectively. The authors guide the readers every step of the way and breaks down the critical processes into concise and easy to follow steps.

I congratulate the authors on the second edition of *Retail Operations: How to Run Your Own Store* and recommend this as a reference for entrepreneurs and retail professionals alike."

VIVIAN TAN, General Manager Asia,
Links of London (Asia) Ltd

"This is one of the most practical handbooks I have come across in my years as editor of *Retail Asia*. The authors, true to practising what they advocate, have paid great attention to mapping out the retail details."

ANDREW YEO, Editor/Publisher,
Retail Asia

"Topics covered in the book are sufficient, wide and relevant to the retail industry. Information on operations topics such as Daily Operating Procedures and Policies, Stock Management, Sales Policies, and Customer Service Decisions are very good Standard Operating Procedures for retail operations and supervisory levels. There are many ready-to-use checklists that are useful even for the experienced retailer. Written in simple English and presented with appropriate store pictures, the book is easy to read and comprehend."

VISWANATH SESHAMANI, Director,
Singapore Institute of Retail Studies

"I have known Angie since year 2000 through a seminar on Retail Management. She is such an inspirational speaker; my team and I have benefited from her talks on retail management skills. Angie has extensive experience and in-depth knowledge about the retail industry. I applaud Angie for her book *Retail Operations: How to Run Your Own Store*. Her passion and commitment to impart her experience and knowledge in Retail Business is remarkable. A must-read for retailers or retailers-to-be. This book provides an insightful look into Retail Management. It definitely offers invaluable guidance to meet the future challenges in retail industry."

KANG PUAY SENG, Managing Director
Super Bean International Pte Ltd (Mr Bean Soy Milk chain store)

RETAIL OPERATIONS

SECOND EDITION

"Retail is an extraordinary business, with an ever-shifting landscape. Being a retail designer, since the infancy stage of retail industry in Singapore in the 70's, I have witnessed this phenomenon. In order to provide effective retail brand image, it is imperative for retail designers to keep abreast with the changes in retail operations.

This book serves as a useful and comprehensive reference not only for aspiring businessmen who want to be successful retailers, but also for new entrants or experienced retailers who require additional guide to further improve store operations. It is also a useful guide for designers who are interested to go into retail design."

SIMON ONG, Group Managing Director and Co-founder
Kingsmen Creatives Ltd

"Since 2005, Angie and Sarah *Retail Operations – How to Run Your Own Store*" has been one of the two standard text books for the Diploma in Retail Management Programme that is jointly offered by the Retail Academy of Singapore and the Institute for Retail Studies, University of Stirling. Our students have benefited from its many practical examples and tools that were based on practices in the Singapore retail industry. In the same easy-to-read style, the second edition has included four new topics, and enhancements to five existing ones. This second edition will be a valuable companion to students of retail management as well as individuals who are starting their first retail store."

PAUL SUM, Deputy CEO
The Retail Academy of Singapore

RETAIL OPERATIONS

SECOND EDITION

How to Run Your Own Store

Angie Tang & Sarah Lim

PEARSON
Prentice Hall

Singapore London New York Toronto Sydney Tokyo Madrid
Mexico City Munich Paris Capetown Hong Kong Montreal

Published in 2008 by
Prentice Hall
Pearson Education South Asia Pte Ltd
23/25 First Lok Yang Road, Jurong
Singapore 629733

Pearson Education offices in Asia: *Bangkok, Beijing, Hong Kong, Jakarta, Kuala Lumpur, Manila, New Delhi, Seoul, Singapore, Taipei, Tokyo*

Fourth Printing: February 2014

ISBN-10   981-06-7938-6
ISBN-13   978-981-06-7938-5

National Library Board Singapore Cataloguing in Publication Data

Tang, Angie.
    Retail operations : how to run your own store / Angie Tang,
        Sarah Lim. – 2nd   ed. – Singapore : Pearson / Prentice Hall, 2008.
        p. cm.
        Includes index.
        ISBN-13 : 978-981-06-7938-5
        ISBN-10 : 981-06-7938-6

    1. Retail trade – Management. 2. Stores, Retail – Management.
I. Lim, Sarah (Sarah Lay Huay) II. Title.

HF5429
658.87 -- dc22   OCN180177309

Contents

RETAIL OPERATIONS

SECOND EDITION

RETAIL OPERATIONS

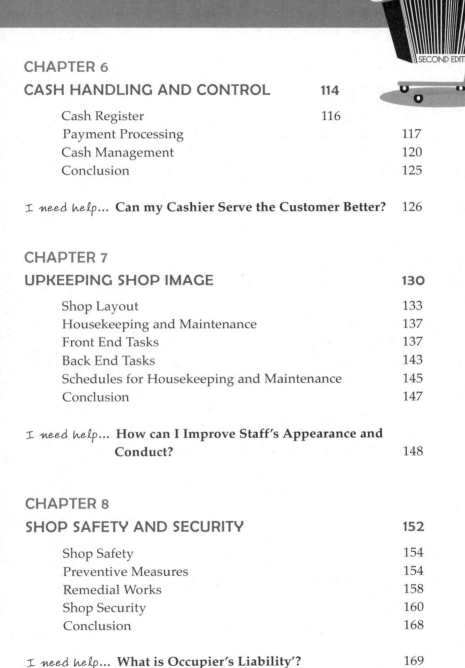

RETAIL OPERATIONS
SECOND EDITION

RETAIL OPERATIONS

RETAIL OPERATIONS
SECOND EDITION

About the Authors

Angie Tang is currently the Head of Retail Management Section and senior lecturer at the School of Business, Singapore Polytechnic.

A highly sought-after seminar speaker locally and abroad, Angie is a key speaker at numerous retail workshops organised by various shopping centres management and retail companies. She also serves as an adjunct lecturer with the Retail Academy of Singapore, associate trainer with the Service Quality Centre as well as lead consultant-cum-trainer at the Retail Promotion Centre. Angie is also a renowned trainer and speaker in the overseas retail industry including Malaysia and China.

Angie has extensive consultancy experience especially in advising the small-and-medium-sized retailers on strategic developments and operations. She is also a consultant-assessor of various nation-wide service quality programmes such as CaseTrust.

Angie is the co-author of two retail books, entitled *Retail Operations Handbook: A Practical Guide For Small Retail Businesses* published in 1999 and *Retail Operations: How to Run Your Own Store* published in 2004. She has received several awards in recognition for her excellent teaching, academic leadership and publication. The awards include the Singapore Polytechnic's "Excellence in Teaching Award" and the Singapore Polytechnic's "Innovation and Creativity Award".

Before joining the Polytechnic, Angie has many years of marketing, merchandising and operational experience in the retail industry.

Angie graduated from the National University of Singapore with a Bachelor of Business Administration in 1987. She obtained her Masters of Business Administration in Retailing and Wholesaling (with Distinction) from the University of Stirling in 2000.

RETAIL OPERATIONS

Sarah Lim is currently a lecturer at the School of Business, Singapore Polytechnic.

She is an accomplished lecturer in the field of retail management. In particular, Sarah is credited for managing the Retail Laboratory and for introducing effective hands-on training pedagogy at the Retail Laboratory. She was awarded the Singapore Polytechnic's "Innovation and Creativity Award" for her contributions to the organisation in 2002.

Sarah continues to be actively involved with the retail industry by providing training and consultancy services. She is a key trainer at various workshops and seminars for the management and staff of major retail corporations both locally and overseas. Sarah also serves as an associate trainer with the Service Quality Centre. In addition, she also acts as an assessor for the CaseTrust Award.

Sarah is the co-author of two retail books, entitled *Retail Operations Handbook: A Practical Guide For Small Retail Businesses* published in 1999 and *Retail Operations: How to Run Your Own Store* published in 2004. The books serve to help the small-and-medium-sized retailers raise their operational efficiency and productivity, and both have been well-received. The books have since been translated to a Chinese edition.

Prior to joining the Singapore Polytechnic, Sarah had extensive experience working for renown international fashion and cosmetics brands; as well as overseeing the sales, marketing, training and operations of the retail outlets in Singapore.

Sarah graduated from the National University of Singapore with a Bachelor of Arts in 1985, obtained a Diploma in Education from the Institute of Education in 1986 and went on to receive a Diploma in Management from Henley Management College, United Kingdom, in 2003.

Foreword

I am excited by the vision our leaders painted for Singapore — a dynamic global city of the East, just as London is to Europe and New York City is to North America. We have the infrastructure, a pro-business environment, good quality of life and, most importantly, a people with a cosmopolitan mindset and who welcomes diversity, to realise this vision.

Singapore is working on every front to make our city a better living environment for all. We are creating economic opportunities, building world class arts and sports venues, bringing in major conferences and events, and developing two Integrated Resorts that will reshape the tourism landscape.

Retail, too, has a definite role in making Singapore a dynamic and global city. Singapore has always been at the crossroads of world trade, and here, consumers can buy almost anything. The fundamentals are therefore strong for the industry. As a result, the retail landscape too has visibly shifted over the past two years. We saw new concepts coming up, such as VivoCity and the Retail Warehouses at Tampines. We are also expecting new and major developments at Orchard Turn, Jurong Point II and Marina Bay.

Moving forward, I am confident that retail will become an even more professional and innovative trade. Our polytechnics and universities are starting to deliver courses specialising in retail. The Workforce Development Agency (WDA) is enhancing the skills of the retail workforce through the Workforce Skills Qualifications (WSQ) system. The Government is pushing the services industry, including retail, to Go-the-Extra Mile for Service (GEM). The sheer size of this combined effort will throw up many more leaders, entrepreneurs and skilled workers who will propel the growth of this industry.

I congratulate Angie Tang and Sarah Lim for authoring this book, *Retail Operations: How to Run Your Own Store, 2nd Edition*. The contents cover practical topics that help retailers to enhance their business operations.

In addition, the "I need help…" sections expounded at the end of every chapter highlight pertinent retail issues. I am certain that this book adds to the effort to grow our retail industry.

Ong Ye Kung
Chief Executive
Workforce Development Agency Singapore

Preface

Operating a retail business is not confined to opening and closing the shop every day. The smooth running of a shop entails many aspects of retail operations. Retail operations are those activities that support the buying, selling, promotion and control functions of a retail business. The retailer must pay attention to the day-to-day requirements of running a retail outlet.

Retail operations include stock management, maintenance, sales policies, customer service and general management of the shop. While each shop should have a grand plan or strategy to compete, the daily operations will determine its ability to achieve this strategy. However, this does not mean that retailers are expected to achieve perfection in all aspects of retailing.

In reality, operations problems surface frequently. The key issue here is to encourage retailers to achieve good and consistent standards in shop operations. Success in retailing is about details and the implementation of those details. Retail concepts, however interesting or new, ultimately live or die in their execution. By not paying attention to the details, retailers are selling themselves — and shoppers — short.

This is the second edition of the book and it is intended not only for students of retailing, but also for potential and existing retailers. The policies and procedures included here are not intended to fit the needs of every company, but they illustrate the types of policies and procedures that should be addressed.

This book offers:

- A reference for new entries into the retail industry who are seeking information on how to run a retail shop more efficiently;

- A handbook for retailers who are expanding their business and require proper systems and procedures to better manage or control their chain of stores; and

- A guide for retailers who are seeking to develop or improve their operations manual. The purpose of an operations manual is to have one major reference containing all the company's standards, policies, procedures and forms so as to achieve better consistency and control.

Some sections contain sample forms written for a ficticious shop called "The Shop". They should serve as a helpful guide for retailers developing forms specifically for their company.

Organisation of the book

Additional topics are included in the second edition. In addition, improvements and expansion have been made on the existing chapters. The second edition of the retail operations book is organised into seventeen chapters that replicate and describe the steps a person who works in store operations would take:

- Chapter 1 introduces the concept of retailing and its development in the future.

- Chapter 2 draws attention to the retail store customers and the ways to deliver services to meet their needs.

- Chapter 3 elaborates on the importance of store location and site, and the evaluation and selection processes.

- Chapter 4 looks at the daily essential operating procedures before the retailer opens for business and closes up at the end of the business day.

- Chapter 5 examines the efficient and effective handling of merchandise when the suppliers send the stock to the retailer.

Procedural guidelines from ordering, receiving, marking and storage to stock take are explained.

- Chapter 6 concentrates on cash handling and control procedures.

- Chapter 7 highlights basic shop layout principles, store maintenance and housekeeping approaches to upkeep the store image.

- Chapter 8 describes shop safety and security issues, as well as preventive and remedial measures.

- Chapter 9 covers the establishment of sales policies necessary to avoid customers' misunderstanding.

- Chapter 10 deals with the extent to which a retailer provides consumers with extra help in purchasing a product and offers a complaints-handling procedure.

- Chapter 11 expounds the steps involved in the retail selling process.

- Chapter 12 highlights some considerations in making merchandise decisions.

- Chapter 13 contains some general marketing practices which a retailer should look out for when promoting their merchandise.

- Chapter 14 attempts to highlight some legal and ethical issues in retailing.

- Chapter 15 reviews some technology applications for retailing.

- Chapter 16 aims to create awareness on issues relating to organisation structure, culture and management of employees.

- Chapter 17 emphasizes on important financial issues such as financing the initial operation, budgetary control, the evaluation of merchandise and the overall retail performance.

Acknowledgements

Our sincere thanks are due to many people who have assisted or provided the encouragement and support in the preparation of this book:

- Patricia Moreira, Lecturer, School of Business, Singapore Polytechnic, for her contributions to the "I need help…" sections in Chapter 4 and 9.

- Mark Johnson, Lecturer, School of Business, Singapore Polytechnic, for his invaluable comments in Chapter 15.

- Thevanathan Pillay, Assistant Director (Legal), Consumer Association of Singapore, for guidelines to the Singapore Consumer Protection (Fair Trading) Act.

- V. Maheantharan (Director) and Willy Wong Weng Kong (Deputy Director) of the School of Business, Singapore Polytechnic, for their support and encouragement.

- Ricky Lim, for his contributions of photographs.

- Tan Hui Ling, Editor, Pearson Education Asia Pte Ltd, for shepherding this book through production.

We also want to thank the following organisations for allowing us to use their materials, reports or photographs:

- **Aussino Group Ltd**

- **Home Executive Store (XZQT)**

- **Kingsmen Creatives Ltd**

- **Robinson & Co., (Singapore) Pte Ltd**

- **Integrated Retail Management Consulting Pte Ltd**

We hope the reader will find this book stimulating, and that it provides encouragement to seek new challenges in their retail career.

RETAIL OPERATION

SECOND EDITION

Angie Tang - Ng Mee Har   *Sarah Lim - Lee Lay Huay*

This book is dedicated to
David, Aaron and Amanda
as well as
Johnny, Alexander and Victoria
for their patience and support.

Welcome to the World of Retailing

01
CHAPTER

Have you ever thought beyond shopping at your favourite store to a business or a career in retail?

Retail is a big business.

In terms of sales volume and number of employees, retailing is one of the largest sectors of most economies. This is hardly surprising as it includes almost everything from haberdashery and home-ware to clothes, food and electrical goods and many others, making the list of retailers practically endless.

— What is Retailing?

Retailing includes all the activities involved in selling products and/or services to the final consumer. It covers diverse products such as apparels, footwear, financial services and leisure.

There are two types of retailers: store retailers and non-store retailers.

Store retailers usually operate from a fixed location and serve walk-in customers. Examples of store retailers that sell products are Robinsons, Takashimaya, Giant, Carrefour, Toys 'R' Us, etc. Examples of store retailers that sell services are dentists, hair salons, etc.

Non-store retailers reach out to customers at their homes or offices by:

- Electronic or online formats (e.g. books retailer – Amazon.com)

- Catalogues or mail order (e.g. clothing retailer – Lands' end)

- Door-to-door selling (i.e. selling by knocking at consumers' home)

"Hello! Is anyone home?"

- Telemarketing (i.e. selling of goods or services by phone)

- Television or radio (i.e. selling of goods or services via some advertisements to encourage consumers to call in to place an order)

- Vending machines (i.e. selling of goods or services by a machine)

E-tailing is a term that is used for retail businesses that utilise the Internet or other electronic formats for their consumer transactions.

Today, many retailers sell their products and services through multiple formats and channels. They not only sell through their physical store but also offer customers the convenience of buying selected products through the Internet.

— Why is Retailing Important?

Retailers are an important link in the channel of distribution. A typical channel of distribution consists of a manufacturer, a distributor (or wholesaler or middleman) and a retailer. The retailer is the final link between consumers and manufacturers.

Retailers add value
to products by making the products
available to the consumer at the

right place,

right time and

right price.

Christmas light up at Orchard Road by Singapore Tourism Board to promote shopping (courtesy of Kingsmen Creatives Ltd)

In other words, the retailers add value to the products by:

- Ensuring the right products are bought to meet the needs of the customers

- Displaying the products for customers to touch and feel before they make a purchase decision

- Allowing the customers to buy in individual or multiple units

- Making available sales associates to demonstrate the products or answer any product queries

- Selling the product at a competitive price

- Allowing customers to exchange or refund a product that is not suitable

- Offering other personalised services such as delivery, gift wrapping, repairs, etc.

"Can I wrap this up for you?"

Functions of Retailers

The retailer performs five basic functions to facilitate the transaction between the retailer and the customer.

1. **Merchandising,** a process which includes the purchase of an appropriate assortment of products and to ensure the profitable sale of these products.

2. **Operations,** also known as store management, includes activities such as store maintenance, receipt and distribution of merchandise, as well as offer sales-support activities and customer service.

3. **Promotions,** include all activities that concern with communicating the retailer's message to the public through advertising, displays, publicity, public relations, special events and promotional activities of the store.

4. **Control,** which deals with the financial aspects of the business, that is, accounting procedures, employees' payroll, sales tallies, customer and supplier bills.

5. **Personnel,** which involves employee selection, training, advancement and welfare.

All the above functions performed by retailers help to increase the value of the goods and services they sell to the consumers and facilitate the distribution of these products and services for those who produce them. The value created from these functions includes providing assortment of products, selling in single or smaller quantities, keeping stocks and providing customer services.

Major Formats of Retailing

A retail format is the overall appearance or impression of a store as it is presented to its customers. It includes the external look and internal layout, the range of products offered and the pricing approach.

The table on page 8 shows the major types of retail stores by product line.

Format	Description	Target Market	Value Emphasis
Department stores	Large stores which are divided into discrete departments selling a wide range of diverse products such as cosmetics, clothings, home furnishings, toys, electronics, etc.	Mass	One-stop store catering to varied customer needs
Supermarkets	Large self-service stores that sell a wide variety of goods such as food, toiletries, household products, etc.	Mass	One-stop store catering to varied customer needs
Specialty stores	Small stores which concentrate on selling a specific range of merchandise and related products	Narrow	Wider choice for that specific range of merchandise and allow brand comparisons where possible
Convenience stores	Small self-service stores which sell a limited line of fast-moving food and non-food items, are usually well located and operate long hours	Mass	Convenient location and long opening hours
Discount stores	Stores that offer a wide range of products at discounted prices	Mass	Low prices
Hypermarkets	Very large self-service stores that offer an enormous range of products under one roof	Mass	Low prices and satisfy all of customers' routine weekly shopping needs
E-tailers	Stores that sell goods on the Internet	Mass	Convenience without having to move around

SGH Sunglass Hut – A specialty store
(*courtesy of Kingsmen Creatives Ltd*)

Robinsons – A department store
(*courtesy of the Robinsons Group of Stores*)

— Concerns of Retailers

Today's potential customer is most likely a savvy shopper with a keen eye for price, service and convenience. They are more sophisticated and more demanding. As markets become more competitive, customers' demands for quality product and service increase.

"The customer is king".

As a result,

Delivering a
unique in-store
experience
is a key goal for retailers today.

The key retail issues faced by retailers in order to achieve this goal include:

Customer satisfaction

Description

Increasing competition is forcing businesses to pay much more attention to satisfying customers. Customer satisfaction will lead to customer loyalty and a higher customer retention rate.

Approach

- Respond to customers' inquiries promptly

- Be friendly and approachable

- Have a clearly defined customer service policy

- Attentive to details

- Anticipate customers' needs and go the extra mile to help them

- Honour any promises made

Offering the right product to the customers

Description

Merchandise assortment planning and buying are critical parts of a retailer's financial success.

Having a successful retail business depends greatly on offering the right product, at the right price, at the right time.

Choosing a product to sell is the most difficult decision you will need to make when starting a business. The choices are limitless. Not only should there be a demand for the product, it must also be profitable and something you enjoy selling.

Approach

- Know your customers.

- Determine their needs.

- Know the market.

- Choose products that you can establish long-term sales.

- Offer quality products.

- Include a selection of trendy products to boost your business but these products need to be bought at the beginning of the product's life cycle

- Negotiate with suppliers to obtain these products

- Continuously source for products that are compatible with your type of business, your location and your market

Presenting the products to the customers: Interior and window display

Description

Product presentation is an important part of selling your product to prospective customers.

Products must be presented or merchandised to customers in a way that generates interest.

The way you display your product can have an impressive impact on your sales.

Approach

Effective display should:

- Attract attention (e.g. by using light, colour, etc.)

- Arouse interest (e.g. by showing how it works)

- Create desire (e.g. by demonstrating the product qualities, use and benefits)

- Win confidence (e.g. by displaying related products to show how the retailer can help them put things together)

Presenting the products to the customers: Layout of products and store

Description

A well-planned store layout allows a retailer to maximise the sales for each foot of the allocated selling space within the store.

It is an important component in creating a retail experience that will attract customers.

Designing the right shopping atmosphere can enhance the store image.

Approach

Your store layout should be based on your customers' decision-making hierarchy and allow for ease of movement around the store.

Each category should be positioned with the correct space and category adjacencies.

Location and site characteristics

Description

The choice of a store location has a profound effect on the entire business life of a retail operation.

Location characteristics include close proximity to target customers, existing or new retailers that complement or compete, accessibility of the store, etc.

Site characteristics, for example, within a shopping complex, site characteristics will include visibility of the store within the complex, walkway outside the store, ambience of the shopping centre, availability of parking lots, etc.

Approach

Before choosing your store location, define your type of business and determine your long-term objectives

In picking the location, learn about:

- The demographics of the site

- The type of competition you are facing

- Retail compatibility, that is, whether the retailers near your store will generate traffic to your store

- The landlord (e.g. how responsive is the landlord to the needs of the retailers)

- Surrounding areas (e.g. will there be new developments, construction of highways, changes in traffic, etc. that will enhance or create barriers to your business)

- Other considerations (eg. is parking space available and adequate, is the area well served by public transport, is the population density of the area sufficient, etc.)

Promoting the store and products

Description
Keeping customers interested in your products is one of the biggest challenges retailers face.

For retailers who want to attract customers to the store without having to have a sale every other month, finding new ideas is imperative.

Approach
Design a retail marketing plan which includes sales promotion ideas, branding and advertising.

Learn how to use loss leaders, media buys and sales events to the benefit of your retail store

Retail technology

SELF-SERVE CHECKOUT

Description

With e-commerce growing steadily, store retailers are embracing new technologies to keep shoppers happy and spending.

Technology has become particularly important when it comes to competitively differentiating the retail experience. Basically, the customer experience consists of three components:

1. Initial impressions (which will influence the customer's decision to shop)
2. Ease of browsing (which will affect the customer's decision to buy)
3. Making payment (which will influence the customer's decision of whether to return)

Technology can be specifically applied to optimise each of the above phases.

Approach

Consider the following technologies to enhance your business:

- Customer relationship management software to gain customer knowledge

- Radio frequency identification (RFID) tags for tracking product movement

- Point-of-purchase (POS) system which include scanners, kiosk and self-serve checkout and

- Web technologies for online shopping

MINI Habitat – Exterior facade, interior design and customer service
(courtesy of Kingsmen Creatives Ltd)

The above approaches will be discussed in detail in the next few chapters.

The Future of Retailing

Retail is an extraordinary business, with an ever-shifting landscape. Many retail markets in the world have been particularly eventful in recent years, with increasing competition, margin pressure, and greater merger and acquisition activity.

Many people have asked: "Will store retailers survive in the near future with the presence of online retailers?" Some manufacturers have also joined in the competition by taking over the retail function themselves. They may not set up a store but they sell the goods over the Internet.

So, what is the future for store retailers?

Store retailers will continue to exist especially those retailers who offer personal services like hair salons, optical, medical and dental care, etc. Personal services require one-to-one and face-to-face interaction.

While consumers love to find the product information themselves via the Internet, shopping is still their favourite past time. Consumers will still want to have the opportunity to see, touch, feel or try out the products before they make any buying decision.

Today's shoppers want a total customer experience which includes superior products that meet their needs, as well as retailers who treat them with respect, connect with them emotionally, and offer fair prices and convenience. Showing respect for customers not only includes having cheerful and motivated sales associates to serve them but also includes having a clear walkway, an organised store with appropriate signage and competitive prices.

However, the slowdown in population growth, greater competition and newer types of retailers, changing consumer lifestyle and spending patterns, and rising costs mean that retailers can no longer enjoy sales and profit growth through natural expansion in current and new markets.

Retailers of the future will have to choose their target segments carefully and position themselves strongly. Essentially, retailers can no longer continuously use the same successful formula to run their businesses. The need to keep up with the pace of change, as well as new developments in technology, simply increases the pressure on retailers to remain one step ahead of the competition.

To remain successful, retailers must keep adapting.

I need help...

How do I Boost my sales?

A key driver of any successful retail strategy is a strong link with your customer base. This includes attracting customers to your store, gathering customer data and developing and implementing winning strategies to drive your retail business.

The other day, I was an hour early for a lunch appointment at a downtown hotel café. Instead of spending my time waiting, I decided to go for a manicure. I checked with the hotel reception on whether there were any nail care salons nearby. Unfortunately, they were unaware of any such salons. I decided to walk to the shopping mall next to the hotel. I found a nail salon from the mall directory and spent an hour in this small salon. I was offered some magazines to read but since I have read most of them, I decided to spend the time thinking of ways that the salon's owners (or any small retailer) could increase business.

First, let me share with you what this shop has done right.

- Their business name clearly states what they offer. When I looked in the mall directory, I saw a name 'Nail Spa' and I immediately knew what type of business they are in.

- They were 'visible'. The shop is strategically located with a bright and clear signage. There is a service menu available on a stand located at the door entrance.

- They have enough staff and thus, were able to attend to my needs. The nail salon that I visit regularly is strictly by appointment only. This shop has three staff working, so they could manage to attend to my request.

- They not only offer a variety of magazines to read but those magazines were of the latest issues.

- They enticed me to buy more by attractively pricing a package of two services. I went in for a manicure which costs $25. A pedicure service costs $35. However, a manicure and pedicure together cost only $50. So, I decided to take both.

From my observation, I felt that there are a number of other simple things they could have done to increase their sales.

Make the Store Inviting

In most businesses, you want your customers to enjoy coming to you. The shop name 'Nail Spa' reminded me of a typical Spa concept with a therapeutic ambience and smell. However, while it was clean, the smell of acrylic nails was very strong. In addition, the owners had made no attempt to decorate or play light music. Providing a visually interesting or inviting environment will entice customers to return for your services. In other words, create a distinctive shop image. Your customers create a perception of your shop not only from the shop name, location, product and price, but also the shop atmospherics, displays, business cards, brochures and customer service.

Develop a Mailing List

As they did not ask me if I wanted to be included on their mailing list, I can only assume that this shop does not keep a customer database. A customer database can help companies keep in touch with the customers and inform them of any special events or promotions. With the information in the database, they could even inform customers if the shop is to be relocated.

In addition, the owners can attempt to remind the customers to come for a nail treatment a month later. For example, the reminder could be sent via a mobile phone message. Generally, customers should go for a nail treatment once a month.

Develop Customer Loyalty

Seek suggestions from your best customers on ways you can boost business. Besides having regular sales promotions for the general public, the retailer can also consider offering birthday treats or monthly promotions to regular customers. For example, during the birthday month of your regular customers, offer a 50% discount on all services on one visit within the month.

Generate Publicity

When I asked the hotel reception about a nail salon, they did not know of any. If the owner of the nail shop had, for example, dropped off some business cards or brochures at the hotel, the hotel staff would have known the shop's name. Generally, hotels are a good source of referrals for spas, hair salons, facial services, nail care services and other personal care services. So, the retail owner must continually find ways to generate publicity for the shop instead of just relying on walk-in customers.

The above steps would have cost very little, yet they might result in significant increase in sales. So, look around and think about a few ways that might add to your bottom line. Successful retailers know they must consistently focus on developing winning value propositions based on the core principles of value, innovation and convenience.

RETAIL OPERATIONS

The Retail Store Customer

02
CHAPTER

Acquiring and keeping customers is paramount in today's competitive marketplace. It is increasingly important for retailers to retain their most important asset — their existing customers. This is because

customer loyalty is the most cost-effective way to profitably grow a retail business.

The challenge to all retailers is "How can I get my customers to be loyal?"

Building loyalty and retention, cross-selling related goods and services, broadening offerings to fulfil more of customers' needs are just some ways of adding to the retailer's profitability.

Some retailers are even going to the creative extremes to gain the attention of customers. Shopping malls feature dolphin pool, skating rink, amusement park rides, etc. In fact, there is even a sporting goods store which has installed a trout pond for customers to try out the fishing equipment before they buy.

With the growing acceptance of online shopping, many retailers and shopping malls are trying to create good reasons for the customers to leave home and shop at their store.

But, wait! Before you think of ways to acquire or retain customers, you must first understand some fundamentals of customers and what makes a customer loyal. Only then can you use such knowledge to help you formulate a better strategy to attract and retain your target customers.

Who is a Customer?

A simple definition of a customer is someone who purchases products or services from a retailer.

Often, in the retail industry, we hear of the phrase — "The Customer is King". This phrase means that the customer is the most important person in retailing. He buys the goods and services that the retailers have to sell.

A retailer has to meet many kinds of customers.

— Types of Customers

As a retailer, you will likely meet three types of customers:

1. Dissatisfied customers who will look for another retailer to provide the product or service.

2. Satisfied customers who will go to the next better retailer if there is one.

3. Loyal customers who will stay with one retailer despite attractive offers by other competitors.

Dissatisfied Customers

This is a very influential group. Many customer survey reports indicate that:

- Dissatisfied customers by word of mouth will tell 8 to 16 others about their bad experience or dissatisfaction.

- With the Internet now, some dissatisfied customers are now telling it to thousands of other people.

- 90% of the dissatisfied customers never purchase goods or services from the the retailer again.

- A prompt effort to solve a dissatisfied customer's problem or complaint will result in about 80% of them becoming repeat customers.

- It costs two to three times as much to get a customer as it does to keep one.

Quite obviously, a dissatisfied customer will walk away from the retailer and will not want to have any business relationship with the retailer anymore. He may not even bring his concerns to the retailer's attention. The only reason a dissatisfied customer will continue to do business with the retailer is that they do not have any other choices.

Despite this, it is still important to have a good service recovery process for this influential group of customers. This is because this group of people whose concerns if not addressed will become one of a retailer's greatest detractors and is unlikely to ever be his customer again.

Satisfied Customers

Satisfied customers can find the same products and services elsewhere.

A satisfied customer is a customer who walks out of the retail shop after buying a product or a service feeling neutral about it. The experience is only satisfactory. It is just a transactional relationship between the retail owner and the customer, that is, the customer exchanges his/her money for the retailer's product or service. Although it is possible that the satisfied customer will patronise the retail shop again, it is not probable.

The problem with having customers who are merely satisfied is that they can leave the retailer at any time if they can find the product or service cheaper, better or, faster elsewhere or if other retailers offer more benefits to shop with them. In fact, today's modern customers expect to be satisfied. Thus, just having satisfied customers may not be enough for a retail business to survive in a marketplace characterised by intense competition, broad product assortment, convenient retail locations, and 24-hours shopping anytime, anywhere on the Internet.

The goal of a
retail business is to have
loyal customers.

Loyal Customers

Loyal customers will not leave a retailer even if they can find another attractive offer elsewhere. At the very minimum, they will give the retailer an opportunity to meet or beat the other better offer. Thus, maintaining loyal customers is a very important part of any retail business.

What is a loyal customer? A loyal customer has the following characteristics:

- A loyal customer is like a friend or a partner. He/She has built a relationship with the retailer.

- A loyal customer will remember the retailer whenever he/she needs to buy something. He/She will buy whatever the retailer is selling and will participate in any event that the retailer is hosting.

- A loyal customer will support the retailer even in a period of crisis.

- A loyal customer is not price sensitive. They will not be attracted by a competitor who offers something cheaper, better or faster. At most, the loyal customer will wait for the retailer to adapt to the competition or offer them other value-for-money products or services.

- A loyal customer will recommend new customers to the retailer. This is a very important characteristic of a loyal customer. He/She will help sell the business by word-of-mouth advertising. If a retailer has a 'sales force' of loyal customers, the retail business will be successful.

How do you get loyal customers? One way is to offer products and services that are so good that there is very little chance that the customer requirements will not be met. Emphasise to all employees the benefits of customer loyalty over customer satisfaction and the importance of forming relationships with the customers first, not sales.

Sales will follow relationships.

Of course, one of the difficulties a retailer faces is to understand exactly what the customer wants. Even if the retailer knows the true customer requirements in advance, the customer can and will change them without any prior notice.

Getting loyal customers is a matter of how the retailer treats the customer. What the retailer sells is not going to change, but how the retailer sells it can make a huge difference.

The challenge for the retailer is to be proactive in converting satisfied customers to loyal customers.

— Basic Needs of Customers

All customers buy things that they need and things that they want. Needs are the things that people cannot live without, for example, food, water, clothing and shelter. Wants are the things that people would like to have but can live without, for example, jewellery, sport cars, etc.

People need some things but they want many more.

Generally, customers have two types of needs — basic and specific.

Basic needs are personal and very often, these needs are unspoken. Customers will not expect the retailer to meet these needs but if these needs are met, they will feel good about doing business with the retailer.

Specific needs are business-related and very often, these needs are the reason why the customer visits the retailer.

In retailing, specific needs can be met through the merchandise (e.g. product range, price, quality, etc.), the shopping environment (e.g. store ambience, cleanliness, etc.), the service (e.g. quality of service, store opening hours, etc.) and the location.

However, these specific needs can be easily duplicated by other retailers. On the other hand, basic needs are not as easily copied, and they are used to differentiate one retailer from another.

An attractive, welcoming retail environment and a friendly, helpful sales associate are the basic ingredients for making a customer's shopping experience enjoyable. Outstanding retailers will therefore respond to basic needs first before responding to specific needs.

A welcoming shopping environment attends to the specific needs of the customers.

Most of the basic needs are service related. Here are some important basic needs.

Friendliness

The most basic customer need is friendliness. Customers like to be treated politely and courteously. A customer appreciates a warm and genuine greeting which welcomes him/her as a guest to the store.

Information

One way to demonstrate to customers that the retailer appreciates their business is to be able to provide information of its products and services. Most customers can do research over the Internet on product information but they do appreciate such information being made available promptly and accurately by the retailer. The customer will be even more pleased if the retailer is able to provide information on the resources near their store.

Empathy

Showing empathy is to identify with the customer's feelings. In other words, it is to put yourself emotionally in the place of another. Once the retailer figures out how the customer feels, they show empathy by acknowledging the emotion.

For example, if the situation involves an angry customer, the retailer may say

- "I can see you are really uncomfortable about this."

- "I can understand why you would be upset."

Most customers just want to be listened to and be understood. They want the retailers to put themselves in their shoes.

Fairness

Always be fair to your customers!

All customers expect to be treated fairly. Customers get very agitated when they feel they are being discriminated. The retailer needs to make sure that their customers are always treated fairly, for example, first come first served. Treat every customer as a precious individual.

Alternatives

Customers appreciate the retailer's ability to provide suggestions or alternatives. Customers will be frustrated if they realise that the retailer knows of better alternatives but did not inform them. The retailer should provide solution options that satisfy both the customer's needs and the policies of the organisation.

Trust

Customers are not concerned about the company's policies and rules. The retailer should not always use company's rules and policies as an 'excuse' for not being able to meet the customer's needs. Customers want the retailer to deal with their problems or complaints reasonably. They would appreciate it if the retailer allows their opinion to have some form of impact on the retailer's decision. To allow customers to have some form of control means the retailer must be willing to support a customer's request or complaint positively. For example, a retailer who says "Yes, we can try" is much more appreciated than a retailer who says "No, we can't". The retailer must trust that the customers will not take advantage of the situation.

Respect

Customers do not like to be questioned. Never doubt the customer. For example, if a customer returns a shirt which shrank after washing and asks for a refund or exchange, always give the customer the benefit of the doubt. Never ask a customer, "Are you sure you followed the washing instructions?" or "Can you describe to me how you washed the shirt?"

— Why do Customers Patronise a Retail Store?

Generally, the most commonly cited reasons for the above question are as follows:

- The store location is accessible and convenient

- The sales associates are friendly, helpful and knowledgeable

- A wide variety of merchandise is being offered

- The merchandise is value-for-money

- New merchandise is frequently available

- The merchandise is unique

- The store is clean and organised

- The store has a good reputation

- The store offers easy exchange and refund

Introducing new merchandise frequently will attract customers.

- The store offers many personalised services with no extra charges

- There are ample parking lots

- There are frequent activities and incentives

From the above list, it is obvious that

the reasons for customer patronage are mainly service-related.

It is pertinent, therefore, to understand the basics of customer service.

— What is Customer Service?

This is a very good question that does not seem to have a consistent answer. Customer service is often seen as an activity, a performance measure or a philosophy.

Customer service is any contact between a customer and a company that causes a positive or negative perception by a customer. Customer service can cause customers to be either satisfied or frustrated. Good customer service is a process of providing competitive advantage and adding benefits to maximise the total value to the customer. Thus, good customer service will result in a satisfied customer while poor customer service will cause a customer to be frustrated.

A retail business would not exist without customers. And if there are customers, the retailer needs to have customer service. Everybody talks about the importance of good customer service, but few seem to follow through on it.

Customer service, whether good or bad, exists whenever there is customer contact or a 'moment of truth'. A moment of truth refers to any interaction between a customer and the retailer that can leave a lasting positive or negative impression on a customer. What a customer remembers about a service is not just dependent on the usual first and last impressions. It is also dependent on the 'moments of truth'.

In a retail business, there may be 10 or 20 moments of truth in its provision of service. These include product presentation, product packaging, payment, product reservation, complaints, etc.

Thus, understanding the moments of truth that are important to customers is the key to understanding what good customer service is. In other words,

understanding what good customer service is begins with mapping a customer's experience

and determining the moments of truth of that experience that have an impact on the customer's perception and memory of the service.

By understanding what the customer requires at each moment of truth, the retailer will be able to develop and execute plans to improve the customer's perception and memory of the service. Customers are then more likely to be genuinely satisfied and return to buy again.

Map your customer's retail experience!

How to Deliver Good Customer Service

Good customer service can be delivered through the following ways:

Good sales personnel

Neat & clean appearance

Able to anticipate customer's needs

Able to offer alternative or recommend solutions

Empowered

Knowledgeable

Efficient

Friendly, helpful courteous

Responsible

Resourceful

Trustworthy

Reliable

Good products

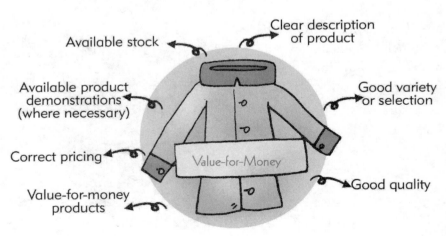

Available stock

Clear description of product

Available product demonstrations (where necessary)

Good variety or selection

Correct pricing

Value-for-Money

Value-for-money products

Good quality

Convenience

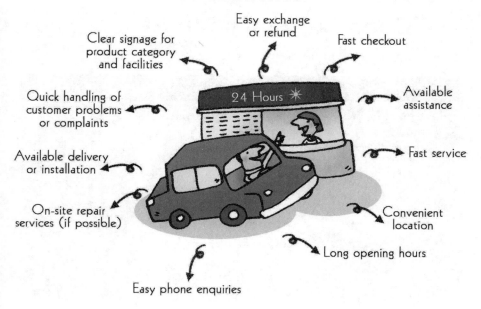

Clear signage for product category and facilities

Easy exchange or refund

Fast checkout

Quick handling of customer problems or complaints

Available assistance

Available delivery or installation

Fast service

On-site repair services (if possible)

Convenient location

Long opening hours

Easy phone enquiries

24 Hours

Good shopping environment

Appropriate music

Clean

Safe

Organised

Good air-conditioning

Good smell

Benefits of Good Customer Service

Providing good customer service will benefit three parties:

Sales personnel	The retailer	The society
• Higher income through sales commissions or incentives as a result of better sales • Personal satisfaction • Happier at work	• Higher sales turnover • Higher inventory turnover • Higher profits • Better reputation • Fewer complaints • Fewer product returns • Higher staff morale • Better work environment • Higher productivity	• Higher productivity • Better economic performance

Good customer services will benefit retailers.

Although most retailers are convinced that customer service is a very important component of their business success,

knowing exactly what type of service their customers value most is an ongoing challenge.

The service that a customer values from one retailer may be different from that of another retailer. The use of technology or customer surveys can help to capture information about the customers.

When retailers are able to determine what their customers want, they can focus on improving areas that the customers find real value, thus enhancing the customer experience and the company's profitability.

I need help...

How do I win Lifelong Customers?

Never tell your potential customers that great service is a reason for them to buy from your store. Prove it with testimonials. Make sure every staff that comes into contact with your customers has the knowledge and authority to solve the customer's problem. Progressive retailers must emphasise commitment to customer service from the top down by establishing service standards and continuously monitoring customer satisfaction.

Many customers describe quality customer service in terms of attention to details and responsiveness. Customer satisfaction surveys consistently show that the little things retailers do make a big difference. In fact, the top two customer complaints with regard to customer service are unreturned or delayed return of phone calls and a failure to keep promises.

Stress to the sales personnel that rendering quality customer service is both a responsibility and an opportunity. Often, the sales personnel view customer service as an administrative burden that takes them away from making a sale. The truth is that customer service provides opportunities for cross-selling, up-selling and generating quality referrals. Quality referrals will in turn increase sales and profits.

Here are some ways to win lifelong customers.

Provide Caring Staff

An organisational culture of caring must exist. The retailers must try to select employees with emotional intelligence (e.g. good personality and attitude) and not just skills. Only those who care for their customers will provide true customer service.

Provide Staff Training

Retailers must have an ongoing training process in place. Try to involve the staff in designing the training curriculum. In addition to customer service training, retailers should also consider training to prepare the staff for job advancement. This is another type of motivation for the staff to work happily knowing the company is taking care of their welfare.

Provide Internal Customer Service

In a culture of customer service, the staff within the company must be treated with the same considerations as valued customers. The staff will then be motivated to do the same to the customers. Keep staff informed of organisational decisions and trust them with important information. This will create a sense of belonging.

Empower Staff

The best retailers delegate responsibility and authority. A culture of great customer service includes the authority necessary to be responsible. Retailers should ensure the staff has certain authority to provide solutions and state guidelines so that they know of any boundaries.

Under-Promise and Over-Deliver

Retailers should never make a promise that they cannot deliver. Keep your promise and do not offer anything lesser. Always develop a reputation for reliability.

Pay Attention to the Small Things

Returning phone calls, replying e-mails and responding to other forms of communication promptly will certainly impress upon the customers. Retailers must learn to always follow up.

Give your Customers a Gift

Consider a year-end gift with your company logo to your customers, especially giving your store VIP card members to thank them for their continuous support and patronage.

Establish a Feedback System

Establish a feedback system to monitor the customer's perception of the quality and quantity of the service provided. Service is not defined by what the retailer thinks it is, but rather how the customers perceive its value. When it comes to customer service, perception is reality. Continuously monitor the service performance against the standards to determine how and where the services need to be improved.

Shop Location and Site

"Location,
Location,
Location"

— this is one of the most common answers provided by retailers when asked to share the reason for their successes.

Importance of Location and Site

Choosing a shop location is a strategic exercise because it is a decision which has long-term implications on the retailer's image, positioning and cost.

Shopping landmarks in the heart of Singapore Shopping District, Orchard Road — Shaw House, Wheelock Place and Wisma Atria.

A store selling mid-price shopping goods such as ladies apparel can be located in a downtown mall close to a department store. The downtown location enhances the image of the apparel store. The department store is a major anchor tenant and it generates traffic for the apparel store which is located near by. However, the higher rental for a shop at a downtown mall increases operations cost.

Locating at a downtown mall may seem appropriate; however, if the same apparel store's specific site is next to a fast food restaurant rather than a department store, the effect will be different. Being near to a fast food restaurant may provide the crowd, but it will be the wrong type of customers and to make matters worse, the apparel store will smell of food!

Thus a retailer needs to evaluate the suitability of both the general location and the specific site when deciding shop location. At the same time, retailers need to know that a location suitable for one retailer may not be appropriate for another type of retailer. The same applies to the specific site.

— Definitions: Location and Site

Location refers to the general position of a shop — a city district, a neighbourhood area, along a major road or secondary street, and a shopping mall.

Site refers to a shop's specific spot or unit in the general location. For example: Unit #01-03 in a neighbourhood area.

— Evaluation and Selection Guidelines

There are seven steps that can assist retailers in the evaluation and selection process for the ideal location and site.

Distinguish the Types of Products

The types of products sold by a retailer determine the choice of location for the shop.

Basically, there are three major categories of products: convenience, shopping and specialty goods.

Convenience products usually refer to goods that are low-priced and bought frequently and habitually by consumers. These types of products are sold in many outlets and little sales effort is required. Examples are sweets, potato chips, bread, can drinks and cigarettes. It is important for stores selling convenience goods to be

located in places with many people, that is quantity of people is important.

Shopping products usually refer to mid-priced to high priced goods that are sold in selective outlets. In addition, consumers tend to compare features and prices, and purchase these goods less frequently. More sales efforts are required by the sale associates. Examples are apparels, fashion accessories and furniture. For stores selling such products,

the 'quality' of people (the right type of people) passing by the location is important.

Specialty products refer to goods that are more expensive and are bought very infrequently. Substitutes are not considered and these goods are sold at limited outlets. Examples are specific brands or name labels of fashion wear, bags and fine jewellery. These shops are

best located **in exclusive malls**
with **compatible brands**
and labels catering to
high-end customers.

STEP 2 Identify your customers

The categories of products sold by a retailer influence the types of customers patronising the shop. A retailer needs to have a clear understanding of its customers and their profile as they form the basis for the factors used in the assessment of the type and address of the location chosen. The following questions may help retailers to have a better understanding of their customer segments.

* What is their age range?

* What is their spending power?

* Where do they stay?

* How do they prefer to travel to the store?

* How far are they willing to travel to the store?

STEP 3 Search for Alternative Locations and Sites

It is preferable that the retailer has more than one choice when assessing the location or site. However, too many alternatives may create confusion as well. Thus the appropriate number of choices should be between two and three.

STEP 4 Evaluate Location

A retailer has to evaluate both the general location and the specific site. Let's start with the general location. There are seven factors that the retailer can consider when selecting a suitable location.

The flow of pedestrian traffic is an important consideration when choosing the location of a store

1. **Number and types of pedestrians**

   This refers to the number and types of people passing by the location. However, not everyone who passes by a location is a potential customer. Usually, very young children are not considered. An accurate pedestrian count includes the following four details:

   - *Age and gender*
     The retailer should identify and count the pedestrian flow based on the relevant age and gender of its customers. For example, ladies apparel targeting at teenagers will only consider the number of female teenagers passing by the location.

   - *Time*
     Pedestrian count should be carried out at different time intervals within a day and week. For example, the peak and non-peak hours during a normal day and a weekend. If traffic count is only conducted during peak hours, the figure will be inflated.

- *Interviews*

  The retailer may also interview the pedestrians to find out if there are a sufficient number of potential shoppers. People visit the place for many reasons. If an interview is to be conducted, it is important to find out the origin of the shoppers' trip, their destination, and the stores in which they intend to shop at. The information will provide retailers with a better estimate of the number of potential customers.

- *Spot-check*

  Some retailers revisit the location on another day to verify the information collected earlier.

It is important to note that

when all the other factors of two locations are equally good, the one with the highest number of potential pedestrians is considered the most suitable.

2.   **Number and types of vehicles**

Similar to pedestrian count, retailers who appeal to customers who drive have to analyse the type and quantity of vehicles that pass by the location. A location where there are many private cars is suitable for a posh restaurant. On the other hand, a mini-mart at a petrol station will survive in a location with both private cars and heavy vehicles.

Another aspect of vehicular flow is traffic congestion. Drivers tend to avoid heavily congested roads. Thus a shopping mall located in such an area will not be ideal.

3. Accessibility

A shopping location has to be accessible so that shoppers
are encouraged to visit the place. This is especially true for
convenience goods where customers patronise stores that are
near to their homes. For locations further away, the distance must
be made shorter and easier with the following two criteria:

- *Availability of mass transportation*
  Shops located near a Mass Rapid Transit (MRT) stations, taxi
  stands with available taxis, and bus stops with ample bus
  services attract more customers and have a constant flow of
  shoppers.

- *Access from expressways and alternate routes*
  For the drivers, a location that can be reached via expressways
  or alternate routes is more popular as a shopping destination
  as it cut down on traffic jams and saves travelling time on the
  roads.

Availability of public transport, such as taxis and buses, is a factor to consider

Parking facilities — clean and brightly lit parking lots in a mall.

4. **Parking availability**

    Customers patronise shopping locations that have ample and cheap parking facilities. This is especially important for retailers who mainly target customers who drive. Availability of parking brings convenience to customers. Customers who buy groceries from a supermarket will want to be able to load their purchases into their cars at nearby parking lots. In addition, as car ownership is on the rise, parking facilities is definitely a plus point for shopping locations. To evaluate the parking facilities of a location, retailers may want to look into the following two factors related to parking.

    * *Number of parking spots*
      There must be an adequate number of parking lots. There are cases where insufficient parking lots discourage customers from patronising the shops. Many shoppers choose to go to places where parking is not a problem. After all, customers look forward to a wonderful experience when they go shopping, and parking facilities can either enhance the experience or give a bad impression even before the actual shopping starts.

    * *Distance to store*
      Many shopping malls have car parks within the building. This provides convenience and shelter from bad weather.

A shopping mall should have a good mix of tenants to attract the crowds

5.   **Store organisation**

A good shopping location is well planned with balanced tenants and adequate facilities. The following factors should be considered when choosing a location.

* *Balanced tenants*

There are locations that provide specialised services and/or products such as medical centres, beauty and aesthetic centres, audio-visual equipment, youth fashion clusters and computer-related goods. However, a general shopping location must have a sufficient variety of shops and facilities to attract different segments of customers. Examples: Shops catering to children, young adults, working people, and families; and facilities such as cinemas, food outlets and bowling alleys to cater to shoppers' socialisation, recreation and entertainment needs.

* *Store compatibility*

Complementary stores located in the same mall help to generate pedestrian traffic for one another. For a shopping goods retailer, the best location is near other stores selling shopping goods. Example: ladies' apparel stores and shoes stores. Similarly, different types of food outlets that target the same category of customers will benefit if they are clustered together. Customers like choices and they patronise food places that allow them the flexibility to choose from different types of cuisine. Example: family restaurants, gourmet eateries and special — themed cafes.

6. Regulations
    A Retailer interested in a location has to find out if there are any regulations pertaining to the operations of the shops in the place or mall. Some of these regulations are as follows:

    - Business hours are fixed.

    - Usage of common areas outside the shop is restricted.

    - Clutters and blockage of walkways are not permitted.

    - Types of signs used must be within established rules.

    - Scope of renovation permitted in the shop has to be adhered to.

    - Malls located within or next to hotels in city areas may require shops to keep some lighting on after shopping hours.

    - Locations in the city area may require drivers to pay a surcharge when entering the central business district.

7. Condition and age of the building
    Whether it is pedestrians or drivers, they will be attracted to shopping locations or malls that are well designed, big, new or upgraded.

 STEP 5 Assess Site Suitability

A good general location is not enough. A retailer has to ensure that the specific site at the location has to be equally suitable. The following five factors will help the retailer to choose the most appropriate site.

1. **Visibility**

   A good site is one that can be seen by pedestrian or vehicular traffic. Shoppers hesitate to go to a quiet side street or an excluded corner in a mall. A shop located at the entrance of a mall or on a major road has high visibility. Some successful malls are designed in such a way that the shops face the central courtyard, and when shoppers enter the malls, they will be able to see the shops on the first and second levels. In some malls, the signs of the shops on the third level can be seen even at the first level.

Good visibility of shops in a mall.

Good visibility of a retail outlet on a street (courtesy of Kingsmen Creatives Ltd)

Position in the location — Shops located at intersection of 2 major streets.

2. **Position in the location**

    There are three important issues to look into.
    *   Which part of the street or mall is the selected site situated?
        Shops located at the intersection of two major streets can bring
        more patronage. A small gift shop located at the end of a mall
        is not going to attract a lot of people unless it is a destination
        store such as a major department store or hypermarket.

    *   *What are the shops next to and/or near the selected site?*
        A snack kiosk situated near a supermarket can have more
        business from the people who pass by the kiosk when they
        go to the supermarket. On the other hand, an apparel store
        should not be located next to a fast food restaurant. The smell
        of food is adverse to the image of the apparel store.

    *   *Which level is the site located in a multi-storey building?*
        The ground or first level is always the best site. As the levels
        go higher, the rental of the shop is lower due to the lack of

visibility. The basement of malls can be quiet and thus, not an ideal site too. However, there are many malls that have successfully drawn crowds to the basement by clustering food and entertainment-related stores in the basement. In addition, there are many malls that build connecting linkways in the basement to other malls so as to increase pedestrian traffic.

3. Size and shape of the unit
The total space needed for a unit is dependent on the types of products sold and the scope of business. In addition, a square-shaped or rectangular-shaped lot facilitates the placement of fixtures and maximises the usage of space. A shop with curved walls or elongated space is not ideal.

4. Space planning
The interior of a mall or location must be well organised to facilitate shoppers' movement. Here, there are basically three areas to take note of:

- *Walkways*
Walkways that are too narrow obstruct traffic flow whereas walkways that are too wide distance shoppers from the shops.

- *Location of common facilities*
Restrooms, escalators, elevators and other facilities should be located at appropriate places and not at secluded corners that bring too much inconvenience to shoppers.

- *Clear signage*
A good location should also have sufficient and clear signage to help shoppers locate the shop units and the common facilities such as restrooms, elevators and the information counter.

5. Cost – Rental, operations and maintenance cost
The following terms of occupancy must be evaluated for each prospective site.

- *Ownership*

  Buying a shop unit requires heavy capital investment. It may be a worthy investment if the real estate value increases. There are malls where all the shops are sold to individual retailers, and in such cases, it is often difficult to upgrade the malls or organise any promotional activities due to insufficient support from all the owners.

- *Leasing*

  Leasing or rental minimises the initial investment. Rental is usually short-term and it allows flexibility in choosing another site. However, the landlord usually increases the rental rate when the location becomes popular. Find out more about the following matters pertaining to leasing:

  - The type of lease — fixed rent or pegged to sales volume

  - The duration of lease

  - The flexibility of lease — renewal and termination options.

- *Operations and maintenance*

  If a shop unit is on lease, study the leasing agreement carefully for the following details:

  - Does the rental rate include or exclude additional operations and maintenance cost? It is common practice for mall management to charge retailers a monthly fee for maintenance and promotional expenditures.

  - Does the agreement include property owner's responsibilities on repairs, renovations and decorations of the location and site?

STEP 6

Use an Evaluation Checklist

One way to help retailers in their decisions is to use a checklist for both the general location and the specific site. An example of a checklist is shown on the next page.

Name of Location: _____

Name of Site: _____

Rank each of the following factors on a scale of 1 to 10, 1 being excellent and 10 being poor.		
Factors for General Location		Ranking
Pedestrians	Number of people	
	Type of people	
Vehicles	Number of vehicles	
	Type of vehicles	
	Traffic congestion	
Accessibility	Mass transportation	
	Expressways / alternate routes	
Parking	Number of parking lots	
	Distance to the shop	
Store organisation	Balanced tenants	
	Store compatibility	
Regulations		
Condition and age of building		
Factors for Specific Site		Ranking
Visibility		
Position at the location		
Size and shape of the unit		
Space planning		
Cost		
	Ranking for General Location	
	Ranking for Specific Site	
	Overall Ranking	

STEP 7 — Confirm the Evaluation

It is wise for the retailer to look up more information pertaining to the location and the site. Information can be sourced from newspapers, trade magazines, the Internet and television news reports. In addition, it is also helpful to consult or speak to current and/or previous tenants at the location and site to find out more information that cannot be observed by merely conducting the evaluations on the checklist.

Conclusion

It is not easy to find a suitable location and site, but it is not impossible.

Simple research and
determined efforts
can make the task
fruitful!

I need help...

What are the Types of Shopping Locations?

HEARTLAND

SHOPPING MALL

SHOPPING MALL

Is Singapore's shopping scene exciting? Many locals believe that there are limited retail formats and attractions here. The shopping malls that have been developed in the city districts and the suburban regions seem to have similar facades and merchandise offerings. Either this perception is true, or we have not explored enough. The truth is that there are various types of shopping locations catering to different customers' needs in Singapore.

Neighbourhood Convenience Precincts

The majority of people in Singapore stay in public flats in the Housing and Development Board (HDB) estates. There are amenities and shopping facilities situated at these estates.

The main objective is to bring convenience to the residents.

- **Neighbourhood centres**
  A few blocks of flats in an estate are served by a small neighbourhood precinct with basic facilities and a few shops such as mini-marts, hair salons, and bakery shops.

- **Town centres**
  The town centre is an open mall which is made up of a larger cluster of shopping and service facilities. It serves the whole estate. There are typically a cinema, fast-food outlets, supermarkets and many more shops. Examples of town centres are Clementi Town Centre, Ang Mo Kio Central and Bukit Merah Central.

Suburban regions

In recent years, there have been a rapid development of both small and big shopping malls in the HDB estates. These closed air-conditioned malls are replacing the open malls in the town centres. Some of the malls are small with a limited number of shops. However, there are also the bigger malls that can compete with the malls in the city areas. Examples of such malls are Parkway Parade at Marine Parade (East Coast), Compass Point in Sengkang, IMM in Jurong and the Toa Payoh Hub.

In recent years, large retail hubs where a single anchor tenant takes up the majority of the space have been developed in the suburban areas.

Examples are Ikea, Courts and Giant hyper malls located at Tampines.

Central Business Districts (CBD)

The central business district (CBD) houses the most important financial and commercial centres in Singapore. It is bustling with people during the normal working hours from 8 am to 7 pm. However, it becomes quiet in the night. There are shopping facilities here, but they cater mainly to the working crowd, so the shop's operating hours follow the working crowd's hours.

With the launch of the integrated resort, the development of high-end private condominiums, restaurants and entertainment facilities in the Marina area and the CBD, the scenario is definitely changing.

Examples of CBD areas in Singapore are Shenton Way, Robinson Road and Market Street.

City Shopping Areas

The city areas are the most popular shopping destinations for both locals and tourists. Major malls and hotels are lined next to one another. Large departmental stores, international brands and established local shops are found here.

The city shopping districts consist of several vicinities. The most popular area is the Orchard area which stretches from Tanglin Road, Scotts Road, Orchard Road to the Dhoby Ghaut area. Another city shopping area is Marina Square and Suntec City.

Historical/Ethnic Districts

Another shopping format in Singapore's multi-racial society is the historical and ethnic sites that comprise shop houses along the 'five-foot' way. There are shop houses that sell traditional goods such as medical shops, food stores, textiles and jewellery.

In recent years, there are many restored shops in these areas that specialise in products such as trendy and alternative fashion wear, accessories, spas, CDs, and lifestyle products and services such as hair salons and restaurants.

Examples of historical and ethnic districts are Smith Road, Ann Siang Road (Chinatown), Serangoon Road (Little India), Arab Street and Geylang Serai (Malay Village), Katong Road (Peranakan culture) and Tanjong Pagar (restored shop houses).

Mass Rapid Transit Stations (MRT)

Mass Rapid Transit (MRT) has become an important and popular means of transport. There are retail spaces available at some of the MRT stations. Retailers can find alternate sites at some of these MRT stations. Examples are Raffles Place (CBD), Dhoby Ghaut (city shopping) and Tiong Bahru (suburban).

Heeren at Orchard Road, Singapore

Specialty Shopping Malls

There are alternate shopping formats that can enhance the shopping experience in Singapore.

These malls focus on a specific product segment and/or customer segment.

These shops are gathered at shopping malls found in the shopping localities mentioned earlier. Some examples are:

- **Fashion malls**
    - Annex in Hereen (teenagers)
    - Square 2 in Novena (young adults)

- **Computer and electronic malls**
  - Funan Mall (computers and IT products)
  - Aldephi Lifetsyle Mall (hi-fi products)

- **Food and beverage clusters**
  - Boat Quay and Clark Quay (pubs and restaurants catering to working professionals and tourists)
  - Esplanade (restaurants and hawker fare for locals and tourists)

- **Themed enclaves**
  - Holland Village (hip eating and drinking places and shops)
  - Greenwood Estate (upmarket restaurants and gourmet food stores)

Paragon at Orchard Road, Singapore

- **Medical**
  - Paragon at Orchard Road
  - Camden Medical Centre at Tanglin Road

These localities and formats are not complete. As the country becomes more developed and global, alternate localities will be developed and new products and retail formats will be introduced. The retailing landscape will definitely be more varied and exciting in the future.

Daily Operating Policies & Procedures

The daily policies and procedures outlined below suggest the various tasks that are necessary for retailers to get their shop ready for business for the day.

Shop Opening Tasks

To ensure that such activities are always carried out, retailers should set aside some time (30 minutes or more, depending on the individual retailer) for the pre-opening tasks.

Housekeeping

Retailers have to make sure that the following four tasks are checked and carried out before opening the shop.

1. **Cleanliness and tidiness of working and customer space**

   - Entrance to shop

   - Selling areas

   - Arrange merchandise displays that are untidy. For apparel, price tickets should not be dangling out. For convenience store, ensure products are front-facing.

   - Cashier counters

   - Backroom (receiving/ checking areas and storeroom)

   - Display merchandise (shelves and display units)

Clean and tidy store entrance
(courtesy of the Robinsons Group of Stores)

2. **Working condition of essential equipment and facilities**

- Air-conditioners
- Lighting
- Equipment such as Point-Of-Sale (POS) system, audio set and closed-circuit television, etc.
- Fixtures such as clothes hangers, display shelves and units

3. **Replenishment of stock**

- Replenish merchandise at the selling floor from the stockroom (this can also be done during business hours).
- Check that there is sufficient stock in the stock room for replenishment later.

4. **Completion and organisation of paperwork**

There may be some administrative paperwork left undone from the previous day. Staff should do the following:

- *Complete unfinished paperwork from the previous day.*
  Examples: filing of exchange forms, stock transfer forms and purchase orders, and update stock information in the POS system if necessary.

- *Familiarise themselves with sales promotions.*
  When staff report for work, they should spend some time to familiarise themselves with the shop's sales promotions mechanism. The promotions will be successful if staff can use them to encourage customer purchases. To be better salespeople, retailers need to be prepared.

Opening the Point-Of-Sale System

Retailers have adopted different systems for their Point-Of-Sale (POS) units — manual or computerised systems. Each system has different operational methods and it usually comes with an instruction manual supplied by the manufacturer.

For the manual system, there is no back-end procedure. Here is a procedural example of activating a computerised POS unit. Some retailers do not have a back-end office, so the POS system at the front functions as the back-end system as well.

Back End	Front End
Computers located at the office for the purpose of keying in and updating of merchandise data	Cash registers or POS terminals where transactions are keyed in
1. Sign on to the system first before using the cash register or POS terminal. Password may be required.	1. After completing the back-end procedures, switch on the cash register located at the sales floor. (For retailers using the manual system, ignore the back-end procedure.)
2. Update all of the previous day's transactions (apply Transaction update).	2. Sign on to activate the cash register or POS terminal. Password may be needed.
3. Print previous day's sales report and file it (refer to *Closing Procedures*).	3. Check that the cash float amount tallies with that stated in the cash float book/file.
4. Activate computer for current day's sales (apply Start of New Day).	4. Record the cash float in the book/file.
	5. Ensure that there is a sufficient amount of small notes and coins.
	6. Activate the following equipment: • NETS machines • Credit card machines
	7. Ensure that there is a sufficient supply of NETS and credit card payment vouchers.

— Closing Procedures

Retailers must end the selling day with the following activities.

End-of-Day Housekeeping

- Report any damage of equipment or facilities to the supervisor and record it in the maintenance book / file for the following day's duty officer to deal with.

- Replenish packing material.

- Ensure that there are sufficient receipt and audit rolls for the cash register and cash memo for the next cashier.

- Clean the cashier counter and sales floor.

Closing of Daily Account

Retailers must set aside time to carry out this procedure. The person responsible for this task is the cashier.

Tasks	Procedure
Cash	1. Arrange the cash memos in running number sequence.
	2. 'X' the cash register/POS terminal and print the total sales.
	3. Confirm the total sales from the cash register/POS terminal against the total sales from the cash memos.
	4. Proceed with physical counting of money.
	5. If there is any discrepancy, record it in the sales book/file.
	6. Get an assistant to counter-check the amount. Upon confirmation, put the money and the cash memo into an envelope for banking, or lock the cash in a safe.
Nets and credit cards	1. Print the settlement slips for NETS and credit cards. The slips indicate the total amount paid by the respective cards.
	2. Tally the total NETS and credit card amounts with the X-read.
	3. If any discrepancy occurs, record it in the sales book/file.
	4. Place the NETS receipts and the credit card invoices in an envelope and lock them in the drawer or safe.
Closing task	1. Count the daily float amount.
	2. Record the day's sales in the daily sales book/file, and the cash float amount in the cash float book/file.
	3. If there are any discrepancies, refer to Chapter 6: *Cash Management – Cash Float, Cash Discrepancies and Daily Sales Collection.*
	4. After ensuring all calculations are in order, 'Z' the cash register/POS terminal. Print out the Z-read.
	5. File the X-read and Z-read.
	6. File all paperwork such as exchange forms, reservation forms and deposit notes (for the following day's officer to handle).
	7. Clean the cashier counter and lock away the cash register keys.
	8. Switch off the cash register or shut down the POS terminal and, if applicable, the back-end machine.

X-read refers to the end-of-shift or sales summary report.

Z-read refers to the end-of-day report, where the whole day's sale are consolidated.

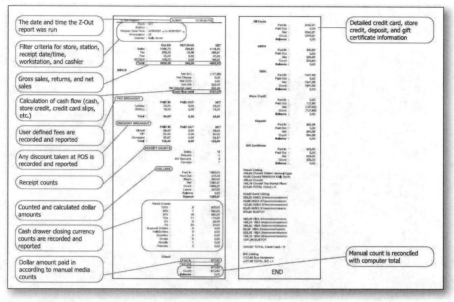

The date and time the Z-Out report was run

Filter criteria for store, station, receipt date/time, workstation, and cashier

Gross sales, returns, and net sales

Calculation of cash flow (cash, store credit, credit card slips, etc.)

User defined fees are recorded and reported

Any discount taken at POS is recorded and reported

Receipt counts

Counted and calculated dollar amounts

Cash drawer closing currency counts are recorded and reported

Dollar amount paid in according to manual media counts

Detailed credit card, store credit, deposit, and gift certificate information

Manual count is reconciled with computer total

Z-out (end-of-day) report
(courtesy of Integrated Retail Management Consulting Pte Ltd)

— Conclusion

A good beginning and closing facilitate staff's selling efforts and enhance the customer shopping experience.

I need help...

How can I Maintain Retail Standards?

Clean and tidy window display (courtesy of Aussino Group Ltd)

People like familiarity, and that is why customers buy from the same retailer regularly. Although customers know that it is impossible for a retailer to achieve perfection in their operations, they do want consistent good standards in customer service, sales policies, store ambience and general safety from the retail outlet.

Besides making sure that the staff carry out the opening and closing tasks diligently, the manager or the owner of a store can play an active role to ensure that the store maintains its operations standards. Here are some suggestions:

Know What the Customers Want

Before a retailer can embark on maintaining any retail standards, he has to find out which aspects of the policies and procedures facilitate the customers' shopping experience. What do customers like to see in the shop? Are they happy with the merchandise placement? How do they feel about the payment methods and procedures? Do they feel that the staff are courteous? What type of sales promotions do they prefer?

The retailer can do three things.

1. Get some tips from the standards set up by the established retailers.

2. Develop their own practices that are applicable to their retail format.

3. Think like the customers — if you were a customer, what would you like?

Be Visible

The management team or the owner should walk around the shop floor very frequently. Small retailers should not ignore this by giving the excuse that the shop is too small.

> It is **not** about size
> but standards.

If possible, conduct the walkabout daily; if not, then at least once a week. Never make this a once-in-a-month practice. Staff tend to only spruce up their acts when they know that the management team is coming. In addition, remember when walking around the store, always think like a customer. Place yourself in the customer's shoes.

Be Concerned with Details

Housekeeping is frequently carried out in obvious areas such as the window displays, walls and fixtures.

Retailers
tend to overlook
some areas that they think
customers would never notice.

These details, if not carried out consistently, will tarnish the image of the retailer and hinder productivity at the sales floor.

Here are some areas that the retailer can take note of:

- **Cashier counter**: A messy and dirty cashier counter creates a bad impression.

- **Floor condition**: Torn carpets can result in accidents.

- **Posters**: Old posters that are ripped ruin the display window and affect a customer's perception of the store.

- **Shelves and displays**: Cobwebs, dust and dead insects on shelves and displays devalue the merchandise.

- **Door and window**: Fingerprints on the glass door and window are an eyesore.

Have a Checklist

It is common to see that the management visiting the floor does not know what they should look out for, resulting in a walkabout that loses its focus and importance. For a start, here is an example of a simple checklist that retailers can use to prioritise the important tasks and standards that need to be checked and maintained.

STANDARD CHECKLIST			
Attributes	**Yes**	**No**	**Comments**
Physical Appearance			
Is the window clean?			
Is the aisle free from clutter?			
Is the display attractive?			
Are the fixtures in good condition?			
Is the cashier counter neat and tidy?			
People			
Are the staff polite?			
Do the staff show initiative?			
Is the cashier familiar with the payment process?			
Do the staff look neat and pleasant?			
Are there enough staff on the sales floor?			
Products			
Is there a balanced stock level — not too much nor too little?			
Are there enough assortments?			
Are the price tags placed prominently?			
Are the price tags tidy?			
Are the products arranged in a logical sequence?			
Sales Promotion			
Is the promotion simple to administer?			
Are there enough posters for the promotion?			
Are staff aware of the promotion mechanism?			
Are customers buying more?			

RETAIL OPERATIONS

Stock Management

Inventory is an essential part of a retail business because it is what the shop is offering for sale to customers.

Customers expect to find
the items they want when they
visit the shop, and when they
cannot find them, they expect
the sales associate to assist them.

If the sales associate is not familiar with the stock situation and there is no proper record of the merchandise, then no sales transaction will be made. Customers will then leave the shop not having their needs met. Hence to achieve customer satisfaction, retailers have to create, maintain and monitor accurate inventory records.

This part of store operations is called stock management. Each task has to be carried out with a set of consistent procedures. Retailers have to take note of the following four aspects:

1.   Area to be set aside for the task

2.   Equipment available to facilitate the task

3.   Documents used for verification

4.   Procedures to adhere to

— Ordering

Merchandise ordering is often the buyer/merchandiser's responsibility. However, some retail shops delegate this function to the sales associates, especially for repeat orders of current products.

Merchandise ordering is
an important role
that carries with it
great responsibilities.

Under-ordering gives rise to out-of-stock situations which result in loss of sales. On the other hand, over-ordering increases the inventory levels in the shop and when there is no sales, the merchandise will take up space in the store room and the selling floor. Rental for space is a large part of operations expenses. It is not a wise move to utilise too much shop space for merchandise that does not produce sales dollars.

Retail organisations have different procedures and rules for stock ordering. However, the following pointers are useful for any sales associate who needs to order merchandise for his shops

- **Know your stock**
  - Check stock levels either during daily merchandise house-keeping or check the relevant sales reports. Some retailers use the computerised Point-Of-Sale (POS) System to monitor their stock levels.
  - Having the right amount of stock at all times is important. Customers should not be turned away because of stock shortage. Know the minimum stock levels permitted for all the merchandise. Once the minimum stock level is reached, ordering should be carried out.

- **Know your suppliers/vendors**
  - Find out the vendors' fax and telephone numbers, e-mail address and the sales representatives in charge of the products. This will facilitate the ordering process.

- **Be familiar with store policies on the ordering procedures**
  - Who is responsible for ordering new merchandise and repeat merchandise?
  - How frequent can staff submit an order?
  - Is there any specific day of the week or time of the day for ordering?
  - Is there a specific day or time for delivery of stock by the vendors?

- Is there any limit on the quantity and value permitted to be ordered by the staff?

- Is head office endorsement required before an order can be sent to the vendors?

- Ensure sufficient time for the order to be processed and sent to the store

  - Merchandise should be available at the right time. In order to ensure sufficient stock for the shop, the staff must take into consideration the lead time taken for the stock to be delivered.

Ordering Procedures

Concern	Guidelines
Area	1. It is important to go to the shop's office to carry out the ordering. The selling floor is always bustling with customers and transactions, and can pose as distractions for the staff. Mistakes in ordering may then occur. 2. Vendors may visit the shop to monitor their sales and together with the sales associate, repeat orders can be carried out at the same time.
Equipment	Not applicable
Documents	1. Order forms or Purchase Order (PO) 2. Price list 3. Previous delivery orders or invoices
Procedures	1. Check current stock levels. 2. Fill up the order form or PO. 3. If necessary, get the shop supervisor to endorse. 4. In some cases, the order form must be endorsed by the buyers at the head office. If this is so, fax or e-mail the orders to the head office. 5. Once orders have been approved, call, fax or e-mail the vendors.

Receiving

Certain procedures are to be adhered to in receiving merchandise from suppliers. This is to ensure that the goods received are those that had been ordered, in terms of description, quantity, price and condition.

Staff receiving goods from supplier

Receiving Procedures

Concerns	Guidelines
Area	1. The selling floor is always bustling with customers and transactions, hence it is good practice to designate an area away from the crowd to receive the merchandise. It is even better if the area is fixed, that is, all receiving must be carried out at the designated area. This helps to minimise messiness in the shop.
	2. As a preventive security measure, when a vendor sends merchandise to the shop, receive the merchandise at a neutral area, that is, away from the vendor's current merchandise displays/shelves.
	3. If the shop has a back door and receiving is done at the back of the shop, then the back door that is used as a receiving point should be closed and locked when unattended.
Equipment	1. Stationary tables should be set aside for placing the goods.
	2. Portable tables should be available for preparation of goods from one point to another.
	3. Carts should be available for transport of goods.

Concerns	Guidelines
Documents	1. Receiving books/file
	2. Delivery Order (DO) or invoice from supplier
	3. Purchase Order (PO) issued by retailer to supplier
Procedures	1. Receiving procedures vary depending on the size and type of store.
	• Big department stores usually receive truckloads from a central warehouse. In this case, the warehouse staff will receive the merchandise and transfer them to the retail outlets.
	• Small shops may receive merchandise from the central warehouse and/or from the vendor directly.
	2. In order to speed up the goods receiving process, a designated store employee, usually the store manager could sign the DO first. Otherwise, the DO will be signed after checking.
	3. A copy of the DO is kept and filed in case a claim for lost or damaged merchandise becomes necessary.
	4. A record of the number of packages received, the date and time, the vendor's name, and any other facts about the receipt of the goods are entered in a receiving book/file. This receiving information may be entered manually or keyed into the computer. The entry should be made by the same individual who signs the DO.

― Checking

Checking the merchandise is part of the receiving procedures.

Goods received are to be checked to ensure the quality and quantity are as ordered.

Checking Procedure

Concerns	Guidelines
Area	The receipt of goods should be done at the back of the shop.
Equipment	Same guidelines as for receiving
Documents	1. Invoice or DO 2. PO
Procedures	1. Check the supplier's invoice or DO against the shop's PO. 2. Open the containers or cartons. 3. Unpack and sort the merchandise according to style, colour, size and so on. 4. Quantity check*: Check the quantity of goods received against the amount on the invoice. 5. Quality check#: Inspect the quality of the goods received. 6. An employee should be designated to sign the DO.

* **Quantity check**

The most common method of checking the merchandise is the direct check.

1. The checker counts the quantity of each item received and checks it against the supplier's invoice or DO.
2. If the quantity tallies, the checker ticks beside the item on the invoice/DO.
3. Repeat the above steps for all items in the shipment or delivery.
4. If the quantity, colour, size and other features of all the items are all right, then the invoice/DO is signed by the checker.
5. If there are any discrepancies, they should be noted on the invoice/DO. The items with the discrepancies may not be accepted and should be returned to the supplier either immediately or at an arranged date.

\# **Quality check**

1. Only certain merchandise requires quality check for style, material, workmanship and so on.
2. The buyer who ordered the goods or a trained assistant may do this task.

— Marking/Price Tagging

Retailers want to display the merchandise for sale as soon as possible. The faster the merchandise is placed on the shelves, the faster customers can purchase the items. But first, the merchandise has to be price tagged.

Types of Marking

There are a variety of procedures for marking merchandise. Retailers have to choose the method of marking that is most appropriate for the size of their store, type of merchandise and method of operation.

There are several marking options that are available for retailers.

Types of marking	Guidelines
Pre-priced merchandise	This is merchandise that is price-ticketed by the vendors and arrived at the shop with price tags already attached. In this case, the merchandise will be displayed in the shop for sale immediately after checking.
Un-priced merchandise	These are items that are not pre-priced and do not have any price ticket attached to them. In such cases, sales associates will have to tag the items based on the price list provided by the shop's merchandiser or the vendors.
Non-marking	Certain kinds of goods may not be marked at all. Groups of products on special offers can be displayed in bins or on tables with large price signs. Pre-priced merchandise from manufacturers can be placed on shelves with the price labels attached on the edge of the shelf.

Types of marking	Guidelines
Computerised marking	Many manufacturers have adopted the Universal Product Code (UPC) marking system. Retailers that carry merchandise from such suppliers may find it worthwhile to switch to a computerised system. The procedures are as follows: • Retailers have to input all information (price, date of delivery, product code, supplier number, etc.) into the computer. • UPC tags (barcodes) with this information are printed and attached to the merchandise. Alternatively, non-marking can be carried out for such merchandise. • When the scanner at the POS reads the block of vertical lines, it automatically inputs this information into the cash register/POS terminal, which is linked to the computer. • The cash register/POS terminal is programmed to display the price.

Information to Be Included on the Price Tickets

The objective of marking is to record merchandise information on the product.

This information includes:
• Price
• Product code
• Department number
• Merchandise classification such as style, colour, model, size/weight
• Supplier code
• Date of delivery/expiry

Not all of the above information needs to be included on the price tag.

There are three main considerations.

Type of merchandise	• Some products such as fashion apparel need more information than others; for example, size, colour and season. • Perishables such as fresh milk and ham require expiry dates. • Small stationery do not require additional information other than the price. • Sale items that are limited in assortment may not need to be tagged individually.
User of the information	• Some information such as date of delivery, supplier code and product code are required for stock control purposes. Such information should be reflected only when necessary. • Generally, the single most important information that the customer needs is the price of the product.
Method of presentation	• Manual gun tags use price tickets that have limited space for additional information to be reflected. • Price tagging can be computerised with the use of bar codes, which allow for more information to be reflected on the computerised price tickets.

Types of Price Tickets

Different types of merchandise require different kinds of tickets

- Gummed labels are used for items with hard surface, such as books and appliances

- Pin tickets are used for socks and underwear

- String tags are suitable for soft merchandise like dresses, shirts and pants

Guidelines on the Placement of Price Tickets on Merchandise

Concerns	Guidelines
Area	1. Designate a receiving area at the back or at a corner of the shop. It is not recommended that tagging be done on the sales floor. With goods lying on the floor and the staff busy tagging them, it creates opportunities for theft.
Equipment	1. Price tag machine or gun tag 2. Sufficient price tickets
Documents	1. Some retailers use the DO and write the retail price beside the products 2. For security reasons, the manager or buyer may issue a separate retail price list.
Procedures	1. Price tags should be placed on the merchandise in a consistent manner, that is, the position of the tag should be on the same spot for all the units of a particular item. 2. Attach the tag in such a way that the merchandise will not be destroyed if the price tag is removed. 3. Important information such as brand names, expiry dates and ingredients on the item should not be covered by the price tag. 4. Retailers who have not implemented the computerised marking system must ensure that the tags are not easily removed or switched by customers. 5. The selling price reflected on the tag must always be correct. A random check by the supervisor or manager may be useful in ensuring this.

Re-Marking

Some products that are not sold at the original marked price requires the merchandise to be marked a second time. Examples are discount prices during sale periods, goods returned by customers and mark-up prices due to changes in cost price. To re-mark merchandise, retailers have to:

1. Create a new ticket and attach it to the merchandise with the original price ticket either still intact or removed.

2. Enter the new price into the computer and reprogramme the scanner computer to reflect the new price (for retailers using the UPC system).

3. Change the price signs or the price list on the shelf. Only the new price should be displayed or retailers may prefer to reflect both the old and new prices (for retailers with non-marking).

— Storage

It is not possible to order the exact quantity of merchandise to be sold. A certain amount of additional stock is required for daily replenishment. In addition, more goods may be needed for seasonal peak periods such as Christmas, Chinese New Year and other festivities. Below are guidelines for merchandise storage.

Categories	There are two ways of storing merchandise: forward stock and reserve stock.
	1. **Forward stock:** Merchandise that is kept on the sales floor near its selling department. For example, in the drawers or cupboards below the shelves and cabinets above the racks.

	Merchandise storage: forward stock *(courtesy of the Robinsons Group of Stores)*
	2. **Reserve stock:** Merchandise that is stored off the selling floor, either in the stock room or at the central warehouse.

Receipt and removal of stock	1. Once new stock is received and checked, it will be stored as either forward or reserve stock.
	2. A stock sheet is required to record the product code and quantities of each item that is placed in the cabinet or stock room. The stock sheet can be placed with the stock (attach it to the cabinet or beside the shelves in the stock room), or filed and kept in the office/stock room/cashier counter.
	3. Subsequently, any removal of stock has to be recorded in the stock sheet and the balance updated. To be more precise, the reasons for removal of merchandise from the forward and reserve stock should be written on the stock sheet.
	4. To save space and reduce cost, more merchandise should be on the selling floor (forward stock) and minimum merchandise should be kept in the stock room (reserve stock).

Here is an example of a stock sheet:

Product Code:				
Date	Reference	In	Out	Balance

▬ Inter-Outlet Transfers

It is necessary to transfer stocks physically from one outlet to another in a retail chain. This is especially so when a particular item in one outlet is running low in stock and the merchandise has to be transferred from another outlet that has stock.

There are basically two scenarios:

1. Transfer of stock to another outlet

2. Receiving stock from another outlet

For both, proper documentation and recording are important to ensure that every item is accounted for.

Transfer of Stock to Another Outlet

1. Sort the merchandise by code, style, colour and/or size (depending on the type of goods).

2. Pack the same item neatly in a carton or plastic bag.

3. Fill in the stock transfer form with the following information:

Information	Who is responsible?
Item code or description	Person who packed and prepared the transfer
Quantity	Same as above
Present location of stock	Same as above
Destination of stock	Same as above
Packer and date	Same as above
Deliverer and date	Person who collected the stock for delivery
Receiver and date	Person who received the transferred merchandise

4. Attach the transfer form to the carton/bag.

5. Arrange for the stock to be delivered.

6. Once the stock is removed from the outlet, update the information in the transfer book, file or computer. The information to be updated should be similar to that stated in the transfer form.

Receiving Stock from Other Outlets

1.   Check the merchandise received against that stated on the transfer form.

2.   If it tallies:
   - Confirm it by signing on the form (received by).
   - Update the stock quantity in the outlet.
   - Display or store the merchandise.

Here is an example of a transfer form:

The Shop's Name	
INTER-OUTLET STOCK TRANSFER FORM	

No: 0001

Date: _____

From: _____

To: _____

Product Code	Total Quantity

Remarks:

Issued by	Taken by:	Received by:	Checked by:
Date:	Date:	Date:	Date:

3. If there is excess stock:
   - Contact the relevant outlet for:
     - An update of its inventory record and the transfer form/file.
     - Your outlet to return the excess merchandise to it.

4. If there is shortage of stock:
   - Contact the relevant outlet for:
     - The balance of the merchandise or an update of the transfer form/file.
     - Your outlet to update the transfer form.

5. Unpack the merchandise, display and sell.

6. Update the inventory record.

▬ Expiry and Damaged Goods Control

A shop's profitability suffers when merchandise cannot be sold because they are damaged or the date of consumption has expired. In the worst case scenario, customers may be hurt or sick after they buy the expired or damaged products. This results in the retailers' reputation being tarnished and even a possible lawsuit. Some items can be returned to the vendors, but more often than not, these items have to be written off.

Following are some tips to monitor expired and damaged merchandise.

Identify expired and damaged stock early

- Staff should carry out random checks on the expiry dates of the goods and for damaged goods when receiving stock so as to prevent receipt of stock that have short shelf lifespan or are faulty.

Set up a schedule

- Checking can be done when conducting housekeeping on the merchandise display and shelves in the morning.
- The manager can designate a specific staff responsible for this task so as to prevent anything from being overlooked.

Returns stock

- Carry out stock returns to vendors as soon as possible.
- For perishable products like snacks and food, vendors often require sales staff to return stocks that have less than two weeks of shelf life from the expiry dates.

— Returns and Claims

During the checking process, any breakage, damage, shortage, excess and even substitution of goods may be discovered.

Some retailers may not require additional paperwork for any goods returned and prefer to have an informal arrangement with the suppliers: either signing the DO first and exchanging for the correct stock on the next delivery, or returning the excess to the supplier and having the DO amended immediately. However, such an informal system with no proper record of shortage or excess may result in confusion, with merchandise that is misplaced or lost not being accounted for.

The following are guidelines for the return of merchandise to suppliers.

1.   Any irregularities are to be recorded in a receiving book.

2.   The person-in-charge or the supervisor should record the items to be returned on the Returns Form or the Discrepancy Report. An example of a Returns Form is shown on the next page.

3.   Ensure that the item code and the quantity to be returned are correctly entered on the Returns Form.

4.   State the reason(s) for the return.

5.   Sign and date the form.

6.   The store manager or supervisor must countersign the form.

7.   Merchandise that is to be returned at a later date should be kept aside in the stockroom for security reasons.

8.   When the supplier collects the merchandise, ensure that the supplier acknowledges the receipt of the returned merchandise.

9.   File the original copy of the Returns Form and give the duplicate to the supplier's personnel who collects the returned merchandise.

10.   Some suppliers may request the retailers to mail the Returns Form to them.

The Shop's Name					
GOODS RETURN NOTE					

To: _____ Date: _____

( ) Goods Returned at Invoiced Value   ( ) Shortage Against Delivery Order
( ) Others
    Please specify:

Code	Qty Return	Product Description	Unit Cost	Amount

Remarks:

Issued by :	Taken by:	Received by:	Checked by:
Date	Date:	Date:	Date:

Stocktake

Stocktaking involves the physical counting of every item in the shop and stockroom. This provides the retailer with the following advantages:

- Retailers get to know more about their merchandise, for example, saleable products, outdated merchandise or damaged goods due for return to suppliers.

- Staff are able to retrieve any misplaced merchandise.

- Stocktaking can be a time to 'spring clean' the shop.

- Sales personnel may also rearrange the shelf displays after the stocktake.

This exercise is usually carried out once or twice a year. The longer the interval, the less useful will be the information. To increase the accuracy of inventory control, certain areas of a store may be counted on a more regular basis such as weekly, fortnightly or monthly, with the schedule varying with the different needs of the individual retailer.

Stocktaking Procedures

Before stocktake	During stocktake	After stocktake
1. Give advance notice of the stocktake. 2. Arrange all stock in proper order before the actual stocktaking day. 3. Brief staff on the exact location they are designated to stocktake and make sure that there are no overlapping areas	1. Pre-number the stocktake sheets. 2. Record the counts on the stocktake sheets. 3. Conduct the stocktake with a team of two staff, that is, a counter and a checker. 4. The counter calls out the product code/description and its quantity. 5. The checker verifies the count done by the counter and records the figure on the stocktake sheet. 6. Use a pen to fill in the count quantity. In case of errors, cancel the original number and initial beside the number. Do not erase or use correction fluid.	1. Arrange all stocktake sheets according to the serial number and return them and any unused sheets to the supervisor. 2. The supervisor counterchecks the quantity with the inventory records.

Here is an example of a stocktake sheet:

The Shop's Name
STOCK TAKE FORM

Location: _____

Date: _____

No.	Product Code/Description	Work Area	Quantity

Counted by:

Checked by:

— Staff Purchases

All staff purchases (including purchases by the owner) have to be monitored and recorded to ensure that there is no exploitation or abuse of benefits. The person-in-charge of the task (the owner, manager or someone designated by the retailer) has to keep a file of all these records.

The following guidelines can be used for the administration of staff purchases:

1.   Create an entitlement form/card for each staff member where all purchases will be recorded.

Here is a sample of the form/card:

FRONT:

CONDITIONS	THE SHOP'S NAME
	STAFF'S PURCHASE ENTITLEMENT CARD
1. Valid only with authorised signature and company stamp.	NAME: _____
	NRIC NO: _____
2. Non-transferable.	DIVISION: _____
3. Staff Card must be presented for verification.	STAFF NO: _____
	VALIDITY PERIOD: _____
4. Staff Card must be surrendered to the Person-In-Charge on/or before the last day of the month.	MAXIMUM PURCHASE PER MONTH: _____
The Company reserves the right to withdraw this card or amend its validity and terms herein.	THE SHOP: S$ _____
	OTHERS: S$ _____
	AUTHORISED SIGNATURE: _____

BACK:

Date	Branch	Cash Memo no.	Served By	The Shop		Others:		Verified By
				Amount	Accum. Per Mth	Amount	Accum. Per Mth	

2. Determine the maximum amount of purchases allowed for each month.

3. Record each purchase in the form/card.

4. Verify the purchase. This is carried out either by the person-in-charge of staff purchases or the shop owner.

5. Staff can only pay and collect their purchases at a designated time determined by the retailer. All staff can only be allowed to claim their purchases after their shift. This is to prevent possible mix-up of staff and customer purchases.

6. Verify the payment and collection of staff purchases.

▬ Conclusion

The procedures and processes for stock management may seem tedious and time consuming. However, with the help of information technology applications (refer to *Chapter 15*), many of these stock management tasks can be computerised. For example, the POS System is able to produce return notes with product information and all the sales associate needs to do is key in the quantity to be returned for each item, and to print the return notes.

Whether the retailer is using manual or computerised methods, stock management tasks are strong pillars for shop operations. It ensures accountability and minimises errors.

Do not 'short-change' your shop.
Inventory is money!

I need help...

Do I need to Adjust my Price?

Markdowns are inevitable to retailers. It is impossible to sell everything that the retailers have purchased. Buyers may have overstocked a particular range of merchandise or they may have purchased the wrong products. Off-season merchandise have to be sold so that there is space to display new merchandise. Some merchandise may become damaged or dirty and retailers need to reduce the prices of these products as an incentive for customers to buy them. One of the most common reasons for markdowns is to stimulate sales.

When customers are attracted to the shop, they not only purchase the discounted merchandise, but at the same time, they also browse and buy the regular-priced merchandise.

Sales signs used on store window and store front to attract attention

Whatever the reasons for markdown, it is important that retailers are mindful of the following issues related to markdowns. There are no absolute dos and don'ts, but retailers have to understand these issues so that they can plan for more fruitful markdowns.

When to Markdown?

There are only two seasons for markdowns:

1. **Early markdowns**
   Early markdowns are initiated when there is either a noticeable slow-moving merchandise or a product that has been around in the shop for a long time, for example, more than six weeks. Early markdowns can free selling and storage space for new stock; cut down on capital investment (funds) locked in the stock; facilitate sales with smaller markdowns since merchandise are not that 'old' yet; reduce expenses on additional advertising and promotions usually required for a major promotion; and allows for subsequent markdowns when the initial attempt fails to attract enough customer traffic.

2. **Late markdowns**
   Late markdowns occur when retailers hold a major clearance at the end of the selling season. The small and/or prestigious retailers commonly practise late markdowns because they want to preserve the exclusive image of the shop. Regular-priced merchandise will not be mixed with the marked-down merchandise; thus, status-oriented customers will not likely meet the bargain-seekers. Late markdowns also allow retailers to create an impact on the event. Customers know that such a big event does not occur frequently, and hence, they are more interested to visit the shop to look for bargains.

In addition, late markdowns, unlike early markdowns, discourage customers from waiting until merchandise are placed on sale before making a purchase.

How Much to Markdown?

The size of markdowns depends on the following factors:

- **Merchandise life cycle**
  Highly perishable merchandise such as fashion and seasonal products require a larger markdown, for example, about 25 to 50 percent, to create customer interest. Apparel, eyewear and mobile phones are products with a fashion cycle. Once it is near the end of the season, the product may lose its demand and markdowns will be necessary. However, there is an exception here. Signature products from designer houses or shops are not affected by season.

  Staple products with demand not much affected by seasons require smaller markdowns of about 10 to 15 percent to sufficiently stimulate more demand. Standard T-shirts and rice are examples of such products.

- **The original selling price**
  Bigger markdowns promote more incentives for customers to visit the shop. For example, a $10 markdown on a $200 merchandise (5 percent) is not sufficient to generate customer interest, while a $10 markdown on a $40 merchandise (25 percent) is more effective in increasing the purchase desire.

- **The timing of markdowns**
  Early markdowns are smaller because retailers know that they still have time to increase the markdown later. Late markdowns are normally bigger so as to stimulate sales of the off-season products.

- **Overstock condition**

  When the quantity of a product is too huge and demand for it is clearly slowing, retailers have to increase the size of the markdown in order to enhance sales. This is aggravated when there is a lack of selling and storage space for new merchandise. In such cases, the merchandiser has to monitor his buying activities.

- **Need for funds**

  Inventory represents a major source of funds for retailers. Some retailers may need to make drastic markdowns to gain immediate access to funds.

What Types of Markdown to Implement?

Markdowns can be carried out directly with discounted prices and/or indirectly with pricing strategies such as coupons and premiums.

- **Sales**

  Promotional and clearance sales are simple to administer, but owing to their frequent occurrence, these markdowns have lost their attractiveness to customers.

- **Coupons**

  Redeemable cards or cut-outs from magazines and newspapers can be an alternative to sales. Customers are allowed to buy specific merchandise at a reduced price when they present the coupons.

- **Premiums**

  Another type of markdown is the free gift and/or price reductions with attached terms and conditions. For example, customers have to spend a minimum amount on the products before they are given the privilege to receive a particular item free or to buy the particular item at a drastically reduced price.

How to Avoid and Delay Markdowns?

Retailers can delay markdowns by trying out the following techniques:

- **Shift merchandise locations**
  The staff can rotate or change the location of the merchandise in the shop. Ageing stock that is placed at the back of the store can be displayed again at the front of the store. By doing that, retailers create opportunities for customers to notice the merchandise. Of course the effect will be better if the staff put in effort to make the display outstanding.

- **Train staff to use innovative selling approaches**
  Retailers can implement suggestive selling to push the sale of slow-moving items. Alternatively, staff can be trained to constantly sell add-ons. Remember that these selling approaches have to be carried out professionally with the customer interest at heart and not forcefully. Train the staff to be familiar with the products and to know the related items that can be used as add-ons.

What Can the Retailers Do Now?

Markdowns must be monitored so that they are not overused, and hence, lose their effectiveness to reduce overstock and to increase sales. Frequent markdowns destroy the retailers' price integrity, tarnish their store image and erode the financial position of the store. For example, retailers who often conduct sales are actually teaching customers to delay their purchases just to wait for another sale. However, it is all right to use similar tools for a markdown if the markdowns are well executed and popular with customers. The important issue here is the execution and frequency of markdowns.

Retailers need to monitor their merchandising strategies and review their buying activities. Have the buyers overbought? Are trend and need analysis carried out properly? Retailers should get their buyers or sales personnel to maintain records on the reasons for making markdowns on the merchandise. These records provide information for retailers to analyse the situation and take corrective actions to detect excessive markdowns.

Finally, retailers need to plan for markdowns. Perhaps, it is time for those retailers who want to carry out markdowns to seriously review the above fundamental tips for successful markdowns.

RETAIL OPERATIONS

Cash Handling
and Control

06
CHAPTER

Retailers have to ensure that their cashiers are equipped with sufficient knowledge on handling sales transactions accurately and cash management efficiently on the sales floor. To help the cashiers, retailers have to introduce consistent procedures on the execution of transactions and cash handling. At the same time, these procedures also help the retailers to control and monitor their cashiers' activities. Checklists for all the procedures are included at the end of this chapter.

Cash Register

Operating Instructions

Please refer to:

- *Chapter 4, Shop Opening Tasks* on the opening of the Point-Of-Sale (POS) system and front-end procedures.

- *Chapter 4*, on *Closing Procedures*.

Cashier counter management
(courtesy of The Executive Home Store – XZQT)

Precautionary Measures

The cash register, when unattended, must always be in a locked position and the keys should be held by the cashier.

In cases where the cashier needs to leave the shop, the next person in line (for example, assistant cashier or supervisor) is to take over the transaction duties. Ensure that a cash count is done between both parties before the handover based on the X-read receipt from the cash register.

Payment Processing

Sales Transactions

1. Enter the price or product code into the register and place the items purchased into a carrier bag.

2. Inform the customer of the total amount due and ensure that every customer pays the correct amount.

3. Inform the customer or display a sign for the payment methods available in the shop.

4. If a customer pays by cash:

    *   Collect the money received from the customer and countercheck the change due before handing it to him. Remember to use both hands when returning change.

    *   Issue a receipt to the customer. The cashier may staple the receipt onto the carrier bag or hand the receipt together with the change to the customer.

5. If a customer pays by NETS:

- Request for the customer's NETS card.

- Carry out the necessary steps to process the NETS payment.

- Hand the NETS receipt and the POS system receipt to the customer with both hands.

- The machine will automatically duplicate another NETS receipt for the shop's record. File this copy.

6. If a customer pays by credit card:

- Request for the credit card.

- Carry out the steps to process the credit card payment.

- Hand the credit card invoice and the POS system receipt to the customer with both hands.

- Keep the other two sheets of credit card invoices for record purposes.

Steps to Prevent Credit Card Fraud

Small retailers may have to consider accepting credit card payment because cashless transaction is becoming popular. However, this may also give rise to more opportunities for fraud. The following measures can help retailers reduce and prevent credit card fraud.

1. Train the cashier to process credit card transactions.

- Ensure that the cashier is able to recognise and process all types of credit card transactions; for example, *VISA* card, *Mastercard*, *Diners* card and *American Express* card.

- Designate the supervisor or manager as the person to authorise transactions involving large amounts or attend to such transactions if the cashier is in doubt.

2. Teach the cashier to recognise fake cards. On the left of a genuine card, look out for the pre-printed four digits that appear either above or below the embossed account number. The pre-printed four digits should match the first four embossed digits of the account number. These numbers cannot be erased by scratching the surface of the card.

3. The cashier should always carry out the following procedures:

- Check the expiry date of the card.

- Request the customer to sign on the credit card invoice in the presence of the cashier.

- Check that the signature on the back of the card matches that on the invoice.

- If the card is not signed, request from the customer relevant identification, such as driver's licence, passport or identification card. If the customer produces the identification, ask him to sign on the invoice and the card in front of you.

- If the cashier is unsure, seek assistance from the supervisor or manager.

- Look out for suspicious characters and actions.

Cash Memo Procedures

In the event of a power failure or at a customer's request, a cash memo could be used.

Cash memo

1. Issue a cash memo by entering the particulars accordingly.

2. The cashier or the staff issuing the memo must write his name on the memo and initial it.

3. A copy of the cash memo is to be given to the customer. The duplicate copy is for the shop's record and is needed for the counting and tallying of sales at the end of the day.

4. When the cash memo is altered, all copies of the memo should be altered at the same time and countersigned by the authorised personnel.

Cash Management

Petty Cash

1. Count the petty cash twice every day, when the shop opens and again at closing time.

2. After counting, record the exact amount and initial in the Petty Cash Expense Book.

3. If there are any losses or excesses:

   - Re-check and verify the discrepancy.

   - Upon verification, record the amount lost or in excess in the Petty Cash Expense Book.

   - Report discrepancies to the person-in-charge.

4. Record petty cash expenditure in the Petty Cash Expense Book and submit the official receipts for purchases to the person-in-charge for authorisation. This can be done on a daily or weekly basis.

5. At the end of every month, the person-in-charge should:

   - Close the petty cash account for the month.

   - Record the list of expenses incurred in the Petty Cash Expense Book.

   - Record the balance of petty cash on a new page for the next month.

   - Reimburse the outstanding amount into the petty cash box.

Cash Float

1. Count the cash float twice a day, when the shop opens and at the end of the day. When the cashier needs to be excused from the cashier counter while on duty, another authorised person is to take over. The cashier has to tally the float and sales with this person before he leaves.

2. Record the amount in the Cash Float Book/File and initial against the amount.

3. If there are discrepancies:

   • Record the discrepancy in the Cash Float Book/File.

   • Report the discrepancy to the person-in-charge immediately.

4. Ensure that there is always an adequate supply of small change for the whole day.

Cash Discrepancies

1. Various retailers may handle the accountability issue differently. This is sometimes dependent on the amount involved. Usually, the cashier will be responsible for it.

2. In the event of any cash discrepancies, the cashier must confirm these discrepancies by signing a Discrepancy Report.

3. The manager or supervisor should investigate the cause of the discrepancies.

The next page will show an example of a Discrepancy Report:

CASH DISCREPANCY REPORT

DATE: _____

CASH AMOUNT (BOOK BALANCE): _____

ACTUAL CASH AMOUNT: _____

CASH AMOUNT LOST: _____

REMARKS: _____

REPORTED BY: DATE:

_____   _____

NAME AND SIGNATURE

_____

FOR OFFICE USE
REMARKS:

Daily Sales Collection

1. Designate an authorised person to do this task (it need not be the cashier).

2. Together with the cashier, count and tally the amount collected.

3. Verify the total sales figure from the various payment methods. Refer to *Chapter 4, Closing Procedures*, on closing of daily account.

4. Record the amount collected and sign in the Daily Sales Record Book, which is kept at the shop. The cashier should countersign in the book.

5. If there are any discrepancies, the cashier is to complete the Cash Discrepancy Report.

6. Bank in the sales on the next working day.

Cash Handling and Control Checklists

The following are samples of checklists for cash handling and control. Staff can check alongside the tasks that they have completed to ensure that all procedures have been carried out. Managers and supervisors can also use the checklist for training purposes.

Cash Register	
Lock register when unattended	
Print X-read	
Count the cash	
Sales Transactions	
Key in price/product code	
Place merchandise into carrier	
Inform customer of purchase amount	
Inform customer of payment methods	
Countercheck change	

Issue receipt to customer	
Staple receipt onto carrier	
Cash Memo	
Fill in all particulars in the memo	
Sign the memo	
Issue one copy to customer	
For changes, alter both copies	
Petty Cash	
Count cash when shop opens/closes	
Record amount in Petty Cash Expense Book	
Initial in the book	
For losses/excesses: • Recheck discrepancy • Record amount lost/in excess in the book • Report discrepancies to manager	
Complete expenditure record	
Complete end-of-month closing	
Cash Float	
Count float at the beginning and the end of the day	
Record amount in Cash Float Book/File	
For discrepancies: • Record in book/file • Report discrepancies to manager	
Check for adequate supply of change (coins and small notes)	
Cash Discrepancies	
Countercheck and confirm discrepancies	
Fill in Discrepancy Report	
Sign the report	
Report to manager	

Daily Cash Collection	
Print X-read	
Confirm sales from cash memo	
Verify sales figure of NETS and credit card payments	
Count and tally cash collected	
Record amount collected in Daily Sales Record Book	
Sign the book	
For discrepancies: • Record in sales record book • Fill up Cash Discrepancy Report	
Bank in cash or lock the cash in the safe	

Conclusion

Cashiers manage money in the shop. Hence, the measures discussed are essential to help them perform their tasks more effectively and efficiently.

There are no
short-cuts!

I need help...

Can my Cashier Serve the Customer Better?

FRIENDLY CASHIER

The number of tasks that a cashier has to perform is daunting. For each sales transaction, a cashier has to key in the product price and quantity purchased, pack the product into carrier bags, sell add-ons, and thank the customer. After operating hours, the cashier has to carry out various closing and accounting tasks. Besides these tasks, he has to keep the counter clean and tidy. In addition, due to the checkout's observable location in the store, customers often approach the cashier for information and assistance.

Do you train your cashiers adequately to perform these tasks?

What are your expectations of your cashiers?

Here is a list of tasks and traits that an excellent cashier should possess, which can be a useful guide to help you review your training programme for your cashiers and select suitable personnel as cashiers in your shop.

Responsibilities of a Competent Cashier

- **Able to use the POS system effortlessly**

  - Send the cashier for intensive training especially if you acquire a new system or when there are new additions or versions to the existing system.

  - Customers frequently feel that a cashier who is familiar with the POS system tends to appear more professional.

- **Able to communicate effectively with customers**

  - There are many types of information that customers require from the cashier, both related and unrelated to the store. Examples are product availability, price, sales promotion, locations of other stores and toilets, news on the shopping mall, and more.

  - The cashier who can converse well with customers will be able to please the customers and enhance the image of the store.

- **Processes transactions accurately and quickly**

  - No one likes to wait, and customers tend to walk away from crowds and queues. Hence, if a cashier is slow in his job, an exceptionally long queue at the checkout will be formed. Some customers may change their mind about the purchase.

  - During peak hours and seasons, get an assistant cashier to assist at the checkout.

- **Possesses adequate product knowledge**

  – Often customers who cannot find the sales staff will approach the cashier for product information.

- **Knows the locations of merchandise**

  – Customers who are in a rush may most likely ask the cashier for the exact location of a particular product.

  – Sometimes, customers bring an untagged product to the checkout and the cashier needs to know where to locate the product to facilitate scanning of the price ticket.

- **Knows how to calculate**

  – The ability to calculate accurately is the basic mathematical skill that a cashier requires. It minimises mistakes.

Traits of a Good Cashier

- **Honesty**

  – Cashiers handle petty cash, daily float, cash and credit transactions, vouchers, gifts and samples. Honesty is therefore of paramount importance.

- **Keeping cool under stressful conditions**

  – Sometimes, complicated situations may arise. Being a member of the front-line staff, the cashier has to be patient and remain polite when dealing with difficult customers.

- **The spirit of humility**

  - Often customers go straight to the cashier to complain. The cashier may feel unjustified, especially if he may not be the one who sold the product to the customers. Thus the cashier must always maintain poise.

  - Cashiers need to be humble and be willing to apologise to customers when necessary.

- **Always smile**

  - Before customers leave the shop, smile at them. Remember that the cashier forms the last impression on customers.

These are not the only tasks and traits. However, they are sufficient to get the retailers thinking. What should you do now? You can help your cashier make a difference. Assess your cashier's strengths and weaknesses, and provide relevant training to increase his productivity.

> Remember that the
> checkout
> is a profit centre,

a place where products are translated into cash. Your cashier's performance has an impact on customer perception of your store's service, and ultimately, on the store's profitability.

Upkeeping Shop Image

07
CHAPTER

Retailers spruce up their shops' appearances, stock up the right merchandise and upkeep the facilities in the shop to create the right atmosphere as well as an enjoyable and fuss-free shopping environment for their shoppers.

The objective is to create a positive image. A positive store image helps to:

- Attract shoppers to the shop
- Get them to go inside the shop
- Encourage them to browse
- Encourage them to buy the merchandise/service

"Store Image = Store Personality"

Store image can also be defined as the overall perception shoppers have of the store's environment. It is the store's personality.

Perception = Value

Perception is very powerful. Shoppers are more likely to patronise the retailer when they perceive that the shop sells good quality products, the place is clean, and the sales associates are polite and professional. They are also likely to become regular customers. In addition, they feel that the price they pay for the merchandise is worth it, that is, they have the 'value-for-money' perception.

Customers' perception of a store will determine their patronage.

What exactly constitutes store image? Some factors that affect how shoppers assess the store image are as follows:

- First impression from the outside of the store
- Merchandise displays
- Lighting in the shop
- Quality of products
- Cleanliness in the store
- Last impression at the payment/service counter
- Behind the scenes: Store room and refuse areas
- Staff appearance
- Services rendered by staff
- Complaint handling

This chapter attempts to explain how retailers can play their parts to create and maintain the store image. It includes layout, housekeeping and maintenance.

— Shop Layout

The layout of a shop is the arrangement and placement of fixtures, fittings, equipment, merchandise, aisles and non-selling areas such as the checkout, the fitting room and receiving area.

Small retailers have limited shop space, yet customer comfort is still important in attracting sales. With these constraints in mind, there are a few basic factors to be considered when designing the store layout. These factors are not conclusive and retailers need only to consider those relevant to their requirements.

Factors	Specifications
Types of layout	There are three main types of layout patterns that are appropriate for different categories of merchandise. • Grid: Use of long displays to guide customers through their purchases. This is suitable for grocery and supermarket retailers. • Free flow: Fixtures and merchandise are arranged in an open manner to encourage customer browsing. • Boutique: Variation of the free flow layout, but the departments or sections are arranged in the form of individual specialty shops, targeted at specific market segments. This is not suitable for retailers with limited floor space.

Free-flow layout of a home furnishing store (courtesy of Aussino Group Ltd)

Boutique layout of an exclusive watch retailer (courtesy of Kingsmen Creatives Ltd)

Factors	Specifications
Fixtures and fittings	1. Use appropriate fixtures and fittings that enhance the value of the merchandise and facilitate ease of maintenance. 2. Proper fixtures should be used for promotional items; for example, bins for sale items.
Customer circulation	The aisle should be wide enough for customer traffic. A possible guideline is that the width should allow for at least two customers to pass each other comfortably.
Cashier counter	Location for counter depends on various factors: • Size of the shop — Cashier counter is placed closed to the entrance/exit of smaller shop. A big store has sufficient space to choose to locate its counter in the centre of the shop, which may also act as a customer service cum information counter. • Shape of the shop — Elongated shop tends to locate the counter against the wall to maximise space for customers and product displays. • Customer convenience — The cashier counter should be placed in the shop where it facilitates payment for the products, that is, preferably, at the end of their shopping. One example is the supermarket, where rows of check-out counters are situated at the exit of the store. Another example is a small gift shop that has its counter on the left side of the store near the entrance/exit since customers tend to turn right when going into the store and hence, come out from the left side.
In-store signage/ signage programme	1. Signage, just like visual merchandising, is a silent salesman. 2. It helps to enhance the shopping experience when there are proper signages to inform customers where to go. Examples are the service counter, fitting rooms, toilets and product departments.

Factors	Specifications
Fitting room	1. It is one of the most important places where customers make their purchase decision. However, many retailers tend to spend more on their shop interiors and neglect the changing room.
	2. The following improvements can be introduced to enhance the comfort of customers in the fitting rooms:
	• Adequate and suitable lighting — Some apparel shops install normal day lights and disco night lights to facilitate customer buying decision.
	• Proper space planning — Fitting rooms should not be too small where customers cannot even change in comfort or view their clothes properly.
	• Good mirror — Mirrors used in the fitting room should be clean and not faulty.
	• Clean and safe — A clean fitting room adds value to the product. Fitting rooms should not be cluttered with boxes or have broken hooks or torn carpets, which can cause accidents. In addition, with so many customers using the rooms, it is important to make sure that the rooms are not stuffy and that they do not have undesirable odour.
Window display	1. It is a place where potential customers pass by every day.
	2. It should be treated like an important 'advertising' space. Thus it should be changed weekly or fortnightly to create excitement.
	3. Windows can be full-back, semi-back or no-back. If the shop is small, a no-back window allows for more natural lighting into the shop. However, with a no-back window, the whole shop interior becomes the 'window display' for the shop, and care has to be taken to ensure that the interior looks good.
Merchandise display requirement	This is explained in *Chapter 13: Merchandise Presentation*.

Housekeeping and Maintenance

Housekeeping refers to the general cleaning of the shop. It is carried out daily. Store maintenance refers to the upkeep and repair of the shop. Note that repairs are sometimes subcontracted to qualified technicians. Staff should know the contacts of the relevant technicians or companies in case the need arises. Maintenance is a routine task but may not be carried out daily. Some retailers carry out maintenance periodically, especially for equipment and fixtures such as air-conditioners and security mirrors that do not require daily checks.

This section emphasises the housekeeping of all areas, fixtures, walls, floors, ceilings and lights and the maintenance of equipment such as closed circuit televisions, cash registers, vacuum cleaner, stereo sets, and more. These affect customers perception of the store, the life span of fixtures and equipment, and the operating expenses.

Keeping equipment in good working condition helps to ease the housekeeping tasks and, at the same time, facilitate the selling process.

Front-end tasks

Both housekeeping and maintenance are carried out at the following front-end areas.

1. Entrance
   - Areas immediately outside and inside the entrance of the shop must be clear of dirt.
   - If a welcome mat is placed at the entrance, make sure that it is clean and in good condition.

*Shop entrance —
Charles and Keith
(courtesy of Kingsmen
Creatives Ltd)*

2. **Doors**

   - If doors are used, make sure that they are clean. Fingerprints all over the doors do not convey a good store image.

*Door — Hour Glass door
(courtesy of Kingsmen Creatives Ltd)*

   - Refrain from pasting too many posters and notices on the doors so that shoppers can see the interior of the shop.

   - Remove old and unwanted posters regularly.

3. **Signages outside and inside the shop**

   - Clean the signages.

   - Ensure that display signs are properly placed and in an upright position.

   - Double-check that information on the display signs are correct and up-to-date.

*Store sign outside — Gloria Jean's
(courtesy of Kingsmen Creatives Ltd)*

4. Display windows

Display window — Quartermaster window (courtesy of Kingsmen Creatives Ltd)

- Clean and wipe the windows. Similar to doors, fingerprints on windows are not desirable.

- Ensure that displays are in good condition. There should be no broken props, untidy merchandise, cobwebs, etc.

5. Aisles and floor

Aisles — Marks & Spencer, Centrepoint (courtesy of Kingsmen Creatives Ltd)

- Do not clutter aisles and floor with cartons or any devices. Remove them immediately after receiving stock or after use.

- Mop or vacuum aisles and floor.

6.   Check-out counters

Check-out counter (courtesy of Aussino Group Ltd)

- The actual cashier counter and the areas around and behind the counter have to be neat and presentable.

- Do not clutter the counter with cartons, boxes, extra shopping bags, wrapping materials and outdated notices.

- If you want to display add-on merchandise on the counter, select a maximum of three appropriate products only.

- The displayed merchandise should be:

  - Small items

  - Festive and/or seasonal products

  - Impulse products

  - Reasonably priced items

  - Link-products to the majority of purchases

- Promotional signages can be placed on the counter to attract and encourage customers to make the purchase.

7. **Walls**

- Cracks on walls are unsightly and can affect the overall image of the shop.

- Inform the manager or get someone to rectify the cracks as soon as possible.

- Remove cobwebs and dirt that usually accumulate at the wall corners.

8. **Ceiling**

- Check that there is no water seepage or leakage on the ceiling.

- Make sure that props or display cards hanging from the ceiling do not damage the ceiling.

- If there is any problem, inform the manager or get someone to rectify it.

9. **Lights**

- Change light bulbs when they are damaged. A dim or dark area can result in accidents.

10. **Air-conditioners**

- Adjust the temperature of the shop to a comfortable level. Temperatures that are too high or too low are not conducive for shopping.

- Check for water leakage.

- When an air-conditioner is not working, inform the manager or get it repaired immediately.

Do not let your customers freeze by setting the temperature too low! (even if you hope that they would buy your goods)

11. **Cash registers and/or Point-Of-Sale (POS) System**

- Wipe clean the cash register and Point-Of-Sale System.

- Do not paste unnecessary notices on the machines.

- If the machines malfunction, contact the vendors for services.

12. **Sound system like stereo sets, speakers, etc.**

- Gently wipe the systems.

- Pay attention to the sound quality. Poor sound quality affects the mood of shoppers and staff.

- When the system is damaged, get it repaired.

13. **Fixtures such as shelves, mannequins, showcases, display, bins, etc.**

- Check that the fixtures are in good condition.

- Clean the fixtures while doing merchandise housekeeping.

- Arrange to replace damaged or unsuitable fixtures.

14. **Tools such as vacuum cleaners, ladders, mops, etc.**

- Learn the proper ways to handle these tools. This will cut down damage and the need to purchase new ones.

- Always place the tools back in their origin storage location after use so that staff can find them when they need to use them.

15. **Equipment such as closed circuit televisions, mirrors, etc.**

- Dust the equipment.

- Check that they are in good working condition.

- If any equipment is damaged, report to the vendors for repairs.

— Back-end Tasks

Back-end areas are areas where customers do not have access. They include the stock room, restroom, receiving areas (for retailers with back-end receiving) and the refuse area.

Customers may not see the back-end areas but it is still important to follow good housekeeping and maintenance practices in these areas.

Failure to do so may result in problems such as insect infestation, damaged merchandise and health hazards.

Here are some housekeeping and maintenance guidelines for back-end areas.

1. Use of space for the stock room

    *   Maximise the use of wall areas.

    *   Full use of floor-to-ceiling height for shelving.

    *   Merchandise should be kept off the floor so the floor can be swept and mopped. That is, there should be a gap between the lowest shelves and the merchandise.

    *   Ensure sufficient aisle width for trolley and bulky items.

    *   Leave adequate space for handling, checking and unpacking of goods.

2. Stock arrangement

    *   Faster-selling items should be placed nearest to the sales area.

    *   Products should be stacked so that they follow the same pattern and layout of the store.

    *   Products should be kept in outer packs or cases, each with its contents properly labelled.

    *   Old stock should be moved to the sales area before the new stock.

3. Food storage

- Food should be stored in containers and covered.

- Cold food should be kept at or below 4.4 degrees Celsius to 4.5 degrees Celsius.

- Hot food must be kept at or above 60 degrees Celsius.

- The danger zone for food is between 4.4 degrees Celsius and 60 degrees Celsius.

4. Security

- All products should be placed in visible positions.

- Ensure adequate lighting.

- Secure high – value items with some form of lock or cage.

5. Cleaning materials and equipment

- Cleaning materials and equipment should be stored away from merchandise, especially food items.

- They should be clearly labelled.

6. Refuse area

- Refuse should always be kept in tightly closed containers.

- Rubbish has to be disposed of daily. If necessary, it has to be cleared more frequently in between the day.

- The area around the refuse containers should be free of litter.

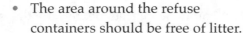

7.   Restroom (if applicable)

- A clean restroom enhances the shopping experience. It is especially important when the retailer sells food items or when food preparation is part of the sales associates' job.

- It is better not to have any restroom than to have restrooms that are dirty and untidy.

—— Schedules for Housekeeping and Maintenance

Housekeeping and maintenance closely affect each other. For example, proper housekeeping of shop areas and fixtures will extend their usefulness, and thus, cut down on the need for repairs. On the other hand, constant maintenance of the fixtures and equipment helps to make general cleaning of these areas and items easier and faster.

Most importantly, both housekeeping and maintenance facilitate the selling process.

Basically, there are six pointers that can help the staff to schedule, assign and carry out housekeeping and maintenance tasks in the shop. In this way, no areas and items in the shop will be neglected.

Areas Equipments	All physical facilities must be maintained in good order.
Action	Specific tasks should be laid out for each area/equipment.
Frequency	Decide on how often each task should be carried out.
Timing	Specify when the task is to be done, whether before, after or during shop hours.
Responsibility	Designate people to carry out specific tasks.
Standard	Set guidelines for each task.

Here are two examples of the housekeeping and maintenance schedule of a typical small retailer.

EXAMPLE 1: HOUSEKEEPING ROUTINE

Area	Action	Frequency
Floor: Carpet, tiles, parquet	Vacuum, sweep and/or mop thoroughly	Daily
	Remove deposits/sticky dirt on the floor	Daily
Signs: Inside and outside the shop	Clean and dust	Daily
Showcase glass and glass panel areas	Clean exterior with glass polisher and proper cloth	Daily
Fixtures: Shelves and racks	Clean and wipe	Daily
Lighting: Spotlight and fluorescent light	Dust	Weekly
Mirrors	Clean with newspapers or proper cloth	Daily
Cashier counter	Remove litter, replenish packing materials and clean with cloth	Daily
Wastepaper and rubbish bin	Empty whenever it is full	Daily
Stock room/receiving area: • Shelves • Floor	 Wipe and clean Sweep	 Weekly Weekly
Fitting room (if applicable)	Remove hangers	As and when customers use the room
	Clean mirrors, walls and lights	Daily
	Maintain hooks, doorknob and lock	Repair when necessary
	Freshen up the room with fragrant spray	Daily

EXAMPLE 2: MAINTENANCE ROUTINE FOR COMMON
EQUIPMENT

Daily	Action	Frequency
Tape recorder and amplifier	Clean the tape head and exterior of amplifier	Weekly
	Depress all function buttons gently	Always
Closed-circuit television	Wipe and clean the exterior	Weekly
Light bulbs	Check for damage and replace at once	Daily
Cash register	Check for sufficient paper roll and ink	Wipe and clean
	Wipe and clean	Daily
Vacuum cleaner	Change dustbag	When necessary

— Conclusion

Treat the shop like your house... you, the retailer is the host, and customers are the invited guests. Keep your place clean and neat and your guests will enjoy their stay!

How can I Improve Staff's Appearance and Conduct?

Shop personnel influence store image through their appearance and behaviour. Every retailer has his own set of rules and regulations concerning staff appearance and their conduct in the shop.

Staff Appearance

The following grooming guidelines are commonly used in various retail organisations:

1. **Uniform**

   - Staff should look neat and smart at all times when in their uniform.

   - The uniform has to be properly pressed.

   - If the colour of the uniform has faded or the uniform is torn, make a requisition for a new one as soon as possible.

   - Long sleeves must be buttoned down.

   - If vest is used, it must be buttoned at all times.

   - Skirts must not be too short, preferably about one and a half inches above the knees.

   - Pants must not be so long that it touches the floor.

- Covered shoes must be worn on the sales floor. For wet areas such as fresh livestock counters in supermarkets, boots should be worn.

2. Hairstyles

- Hair should be neat, clean and worn in a professional manner.
- Fanciful and elaborate hairstyles should be avoided.
- Long hair (touching the shoulder or longer) should be tied back or knotted into a 'bun'.
- Long hair may also be combed back away from the forehead and secured with a black headband or hair clip.
- The few strands of hair that are too short to be tied up should be tidied up with a little gel.
- Overall, hair should not cover any part of the eyes or be a hindrance to work.
- Coloured hair should be restricted to black or brown tones similar to the staff's original hair color.

3. Hair-accessories

- All hair accessories should be in the colour similar to the staff's hair colour.

4. Fashion accessories

- Accessories should be small and simple.
- There should not be too many items.
- They should not obstruct work and cause inconvenience.

5. Make-up

- Light make-up can be worn.

6. **Nails**

    - Nails should be kept short and neatly trimmed.

    - If nail polish is used, the colour should be neutral and not too bright.

    - Do not have nail extension or fancifully patterned nails. This is very important for sales associates who need to handle food.

7. **Hygiene**

    - Comply with sanitation requirements when handling food in the shop.

    - Observe personal hygiene and cleanliness.

    - Do not use strong perfumes or fragrance.

Staff Conduct

Shoppers observe staff behaviours even before they enter the shop. Hence, it is necessary that staff be mindful of their conduct at all times.

Generally, staff have to be mindful of the following behaviours.

1. **Chatting among themselves**

    - Shoppers are often turned off when staff talk among themselves and ignore them.

2. **Talking loudly or shouting**

    - Sometimes, staff may get carried away and talk and/or joke loudly with each other or the customers.

3. **Eating and drinking**

    - Eating in the shop causes the shop to smell. This is especially true when staff consume food with strong smells.

- In cases where there is only one staff in the shop, allowing staff to lunch inside the shop may be necessary. Staff should only eat food that are not strong in smell or with too much sauce, such as sandwiches. In addition, efforts must be made to refresh the scent in the shop, such as spraying fragrances or perfumes.

4. **Doing paperwork on the counter top**

- Sales staff who are too engrossed doing their paperwork on the counter top tend to ignore customers inside the shop. This not only results in loss of sales and creating a bad impression, but also encourages shoplifting.

5. **Attitude towards customers**

- Staff encounter different customers daily. They have different needs and like to be served in different manners. Hence, staff should have a positive attitude when dealing with customers. They should exhibit the following attributes:

  - Polite: Even when dealing with unreasonable customers

  - Friendly: Lower customers' resistance to buy

  - Use eye contact: Shows that you care and listen

  - Listen attentively: Find out customers' immediate needs

  - Rephrase what customers say: To be sure of their requests and to seek their approval

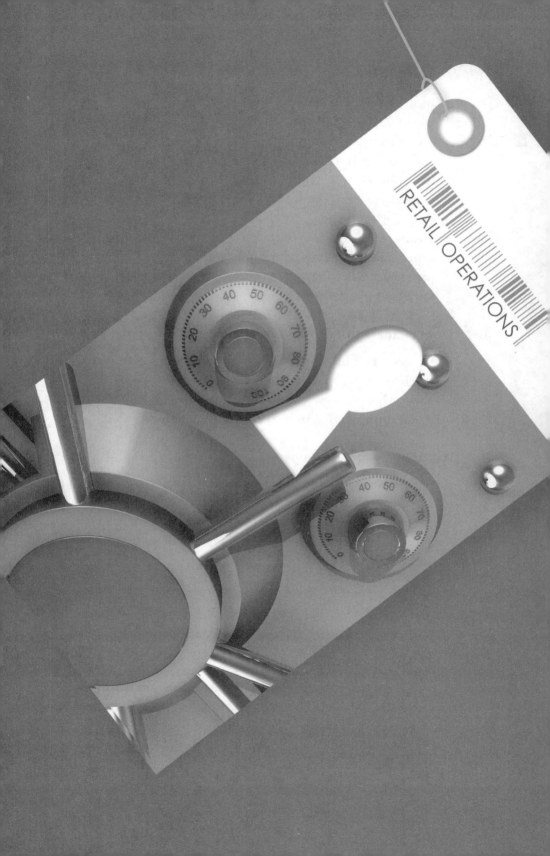

Shop Safety and Security

The main objective of opening a shop is to invite shoppers into the premises to browse and buy. Retailers clean their shops, arrange the fixtures properly and beautify the displays to create a good impression so as to make sure that shoppers feel comfortable inside their shops. Is there anything else retailers need to do?

— Shop Safety

Retailers have to ensure the safety of shoppers in the shop. Shoppers, too, expect the retailers to provide a hazard-free shopping environment.

Accidents generate bad publicity for retailers.

Once shoppers know that a particular shop is prone to accidents, they avoid the place and choose to shop somewhere else. Even if an accident occurs only once, shoppers will avoid the place for a period of time before they resume their shopping there. In both cases, the shop's reputation is tarnished.

What about the employees? It is also the retailer's responsibility to ensure the safety of the staff working on the premises.

— Preventive measures

Prevention is better than cure. Some of the preventive measures are discussed below.

Staff's responsibilities

1.   Have a 'safety first' attitude

   • Staff may not be able to anticipate every accident but they can help to prevent most of it.

- Accidents cost money and bring inconvenience to shoppers and staff. In serious cases, accidents can result in injuries and even death.

- Having a 'safety first' attitude is a good start to prevent accidents. Every time you need to do something, think of safety first.

2. Keep a lookout for dangerous signs

- Be aware of situations that are hazardous and take actions to rectify them.

- Some examples are:

    - Empty boxes on aisles

    - Defective fixtures such as broken glass or chipped fixtures

    - Shelves with overloaded merchandise

    - Torn carpets that can cause shoppers to trip

    - High displays that may topple

    - Overused electric outlets

    - Dangling electrical cords from appliances

    - Fallen merchandise and / or packaging materials on the floor

    - Wet floor

    - Sharp corners on display units

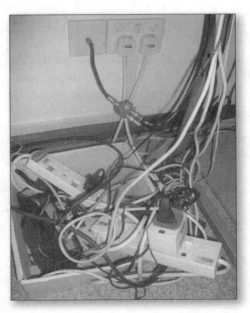

Fire hazards: dangling wires and overloaded socket points (courtesy of Agnes Lim)

3. **Pay attention to activities and events going on in the shop**

- Be alert to incidents that are potential grounds for accidents. Some examples are:

  - Children running around in the shop

  - Children playing with trolleys (in supermarkets)

  - Influx of customers during sales periods

  - Crowds building up at certain counters and departments

4. **Use the right tools**

- Tools are often used to facilitate the sales associate's jobs, whether receiving stocks, cleaning the floor, replenishing merchandise or putting up displays.

- Learn the correct ways to use the tools.

- Use the correct tools to do the work. Examples are:

  - Use a step ladder to retrieve or put items placed on high shelves or displays that are out of reach. Do not substitute a step ladder with cartons or crates.

  - Use a trolley to transfer goods from one place to another.

  - Use appropriate lifting equipment to lift heavy items.

  - Wear protective gloves when handling hot food.

  - Put on rubber boots if you need to work on a wet floor (e.g. a seafood department in supermarket).

5. **Report safety problems in the shop**

- It is important to highlight safety problems to the management so that rectifications can be made before accidents happen.

- Staff should have a positive attitude towards this and not be apprehensive about reporting because of fear of more work or inconvenience.

Tips to Prevent Fire Hazards

- Ensure that the main power point is turned off at closing.

- Customers should not be allowed to smoke in the shop.

- Staff should be aware of the location of fire extinguishers.

- Staff should be trained in the use of fire extinguishers, be aware of the location of the alarms and be familiar with emergency evacuation procedures.

- Ensure that exits are not locked or blocked during opening hours.

Tips to Prevent Occurrence of Accidents

- Torn carpeting, protruding counters or displays, slippery floors and other potential dangers should be reported promptly and then repaired or rectified.

- The safety of areas inside the shop and immediately outside the shop should also be included.

- All accidents that happened to customers and staff should be recorded in an accident log and, if necessary, a report should be sent to the relevant authorities.

- First aid facilities should be provided and the supplies should be in usable condition. Staff should also know the location of the first aid supplies.

- In the case of minor customer accidents, staff should help to relieve pain or ease the inconvenience suffered. Any major injuries, however, should be left to medical professionals.

▬ Remedial works

Some shops have maintenance personnel to fix damaged fixtures, clean up spills and pick up broken glasses. In other shops, sales associates are required to perform such tasks. Whatever the case, different retailers observe different sets of procedures and practices when safety hazards occur. Some of the common practices are discussed below.

Procedures When Safety Hazards Occur

1. Put up a sign or barrier (yellow caution signs or orange safety cones) to keep customers away from the accident area.

2. If possible, a staff should be stationed at the accident site until the problem is resolved. Staff should warn customers to avoid the problem area.

3. Call maintenance or the manager for help if appropriate; if not, rectify the problem without delay.

4. If the problem is not major and if staff are able to do so, make minor repairs or correct the situation while waiting for help.

Procedures When A Customer is Injured

1. First and foremost, staff have to be familiar with store policies and procedures that are in place because accidents happen unexpectedly and staff need to respond quickly.

2. Don't panic, remain calm. Staff should get a clear idea of what has happened and the extent of injury so that they can decide on the follow-up actions.

3. Attend to the customer first. Check the victim's condition.

4. Know where the first aid kit is. It should be placed near the cash register.

5. Know what to do and what not to do to relieve the customer's pain and discomfort.

    - Keep an injured person lying down.

    - Perform CPR (Cardiopulmonary Resuscitation) if necessary. If staff are not able to do so, make sure they know the staff who knows how to do it and call for that person to help.

    - Do not let shoppers crowd around the victim as he needs fresh air.

    - Do not touch the victim since staff may not know where the injury is.

    - Do not move the victim as the movement may cause further injury.

    - Do not give the victim any form of drug. Some people are allergic even to aspirin.

6. Notify shop security or the management.

7. Call the relevant authorities for help. Staff should keep a list of emergency contact numbers of relevant authorities. The numbers should be placed at the check out counters.

8. Provide accurate reports when required.

   • Staff may be required to fill out a written form.

   • File the reports for future reference and training purposes.

There are many more safety issues and guidelines that a sale associate can find out about the workplace. Some retailers have elaborate practices and procedures but the smaller shops may not have a comprehensive plan. In either case, staff can take initiatives to apply common sense and good judgment to resolve the problems when safety hazards occur. When there is a will, there will be a way.

— Shop security

Theft by customers and staff reduces a retailer's profit by a great extent. Retailers must employ effective measures and loss control equipment to keep losses to a minimum. These measures and equipments are primarily preventive in nature — they are instituted to deter theft and not to catch shoplifters.

Shoplifting

The methods used to combat shoplifting can be divided into two main categories: measures and equipment.

1. **Detective and preventive measures**

- If a staff is not sure whether a customer has committed theft, it is better to let the suspect go. If the suspect has nothing in his possession but is wrongly accused, this would imply a wrongful arrest. The customer can then sue the shop and the reputation of the shop would be affected.

- The apprehension procedures to follow when a staff witness a theft:

  - Inform the store manager and keep the suspect under constant observation (because the shoplifter may replace an item that the staff has seen him/her take or dispose of it in such a way that the staff may not be aware of).

  - The manager or the person in-charge of the shop should be responsible for apprehension. But if the manager is not in the shop or there is no senior staff around, then the staff will have to carry out the apprehension.

  - A shoplifter can only be apprehended after he leaves the shop. Some customers may still be browsing and actually have the intention to pay.

  - Approach the suspect tactfully by saying, "Excuse me, Sir/Madam, you have not paid for the items. Would you like to do so?" At the same time, direct him to the cashier counter.

Sometimes, a customer will react violently to your allegations of shoplifting.

- If the suspect denies taking anything:

  - ◆ Do not threaten the suspect or make unnecessary remarks because the suspect can use them against the staff.

  - ◆ Do not use force except in self-defence.

  - ◆ Never touch or physically search the suspect.

  - ◆ Try to detain the suspect and call for help.

- If the suspect breaks away and runs, do not give chase. The suspect may have conspired with another person and while there is a commotion during the chase, the accomplice can easily take more items away from the shop.

- If the suspect cooperates, bring him to the office (away from the public as privacy is important).

  - ◆ Be polite throughout the ordeal (no threats, no force, no physical search).

  - ◆ Try to recover the merchandise.

  - ◆ Have a store employee who is of the same sex as the suspect in the office at all times to avoid potential trouble.

  - ◆ Try to obtain a written statement from the suspect. Ensure that he signs it and the person-in-charge signs it as a witness.

- A warning should be given to the suspect. In serious cases, a police report may be made. However, in some minor cases, a verbal or written warning may be sufficient.

- Retailers should keep a record of all such cases.

2. Loss control equipment

Loss control equipment does not fully protect against theft but it can be used as a psychological deterrence. However, for it to be effective, all staff have to be trained in its use and maintenance.

Closed-circuit television

Security mirror
(courtesy of Integrated Retail
Management Consulting
Pte Ltd)

Electronic article surveillance panel (courtesy of Kingsmen Creatives Ltd)

The following are some examples that retailers may want to consider.

- Closed-circuit television
- Electronic article surveillance: Wafer-like electronic or magnetic tag together with the monitoring panels
- Ink tags: Do not require the monitoring panels
- Security mirrors: Convex mirrors, one-way mirrors
- Showcase locks
- Chains
- Fitting room tags
- Intruder alarm (outside opening hours)

Staff Pilferage

Staff pilferage refers to the direct theft of stock or cash by a shop employee. It can be committed either by an individual staff member or through the collaboration between staff and delivery personnel, salespersons or customers. The following are areas that are prone to staff pilferage:

- Cashier counter where theft from tills and dishonesty with floats, petty cash and banking can occur

- Goods receiving area

- Stock room

For internal security, the following precautions should be taken:

Areas	Precaution
Sales floor/ Cashier counter	• Employees' handbags and belongings should be left in a separate room or kept away from the sales floor.
	• Separate staff purchases from the customer sales system. Retailers may want to administer staff purchases on a designated day and time only.
	• Employ an honest shopper as undercover personnel to check that the sales staff and cashiers perform their duties according to shop policies and procedures.
	• Instruct and train cashiers to carry out proper handover and cashing procedures.
	• Spot check tills from the cash register audit rolls.
	• Designate staff, usually the manager, to sign all credit notes, refunds and exchanges.
Stock room	• Lock away all expensive merchandise.
	• Keep merchandise in sealed outer packaging.
	• Ensure that staff carry out procedures for stock transfers and stock checks.
Goods receiving area	• Identify delivery personnel. Record their particulars and company names.
	• Train staff on the correct acceptance procedure for deliveries.

Restricted Areas

A shop is an open area where customers are encouraged to enter to browse. However, there should be restricted areas within the shop where customers or friends of staff are strictly not allowed to enter. These areas are:

1. Inside the cashier counter

2. Inside the stockroom

3. Inside the receiving area

Power Failure/Blackout

In the event of a power failure, customers may still be in the shop. Staff have to ensure that no merchandise or cash is taken away.

1. Staff must immediately be stationed at the entrance to stop all incoming customers, informing them politely of the power failure.

2. Staff must be stationed inside the shop to help customers leave the shop.

3. Close entrances other than the main one where possible.

4. The cashier must guard the cash register.

5. All sales transactions must stop.

6. Allow customers to leave the shop only after checking their belongings. This must be handled tactfully.

Circulation and Control of Keys

Improper management of keys tempts staff to steal. Retailers must implement strict key circulation for the following areas.

Areas	Precautions
Cash register and drawer	1. The cash drawer must be locked at all times. 2. The cash register must be locked and the key kept in the cash drawer when not in use. 3. For procedures when the cashier has to leave the shop during duty hours, refer to Section 6.1, Cash Register.
Showcase cabinets and cupboards	1. Designate staff to safekeep all keys. This task may require more than one employee to cover all shifts. 2. Sales staff in charge of the particular display cabinet is to be given the responsibility of safeguarding the key. This is to facilitate selling of goods. 3. All showcases, cupboards and cabinets housing expensive merchandise must be locked at all times. 4. When the authorised staff has to leave the store, the assistant should take over the keys. 5. Open the showcase only when customers need to inspect or buy the merchandise. The keys should not be left out in the open. 6. Daily stock checks should be carried out for high-value merchandise that is kept under lock and key. Sales staff, together with the supervisor or manager, can assume this responsibility.

Areas	Precautions
Shop keys	1. All entrance and backdoor keys, if applicable, must be attached together and held by the person-in-charge (most likely the owner).
Important considerations	1. No key should be left out in the open. 2. Any authorised staff holding the keys (cashiers, managers or even sales staff) must be fully accountable for the safekeeping of the keys. 3. If any set of keys is lost or temporarily misplaced and later found, the set of keys and locks has to be replaced.

Robbery

There are two concerns to be taken into account when developing any robbery security programme. The retailer's first concern is to train the employees on how to handle an actual robbery situation. Second, the retailer should introduce preventive measures to minimise loss in the case of robbery.

Procedures and instructions in an actual robbery situation

1. Remain calm.

2. Do not make any sudden moves.

3. Reassure the robbers that they can expect full cooperation in every way.

4. Make no attempt to apprehend the robbers.

5. Give the robbers whatever they want.

6. Attempt to make a mental note of the robber's description (height, hairstyle, eye colour, voice, complexion, clothing and so on).

7. Keep still until the robbers have left the premises.

8. Call the police.

9. Talk only to the police and the store manager about the situation.

Do not try to fight the robber! (As this is probably what will not happen.)

Preventive measures

1. Keep as little cash in the cash register as possible. Remove excess cash frequently.

2. Maintain a minimum level of operating cash and bank all excess cash.

3. Vary bank trip routes and times.

4. Keep shop safes locked at all times.

5. Get two persons to open and close the shop — one for the actual opening and closing of the shop and the other to keep watch outside.

Conclusion

There are two main objectives: to prevent the occurrence of conditions that can cause harm to customers and staff, and to minimise inventory and money losses. All staff should be educated on the precautionary measures and corrective procedures to be adopted.

I need help...

What is 'Occupier's Liability'?

An attractive store layout may tempt buyers to enter a store and make purchases that keep the cash registers ringing. Good store lighting will allow the goods to look their best. Attractive decor and tasteful piped music will make the shopping experience a pleasant one for customers.

A prudent retailer, however, would do well to look beyond just providing a pleasant shopping environment for customers. He would ensure that the shop premises are maintained in a reasonably safe condition. Although few people realise it, shop premises are fertile ground for accidents. Some water on the floor may cause an unsuspecting shopper to slip and fall, perhaps bringing the goods tumbling down on the customer; staff rushing around may collide into shoppers, and the list goes on.

The law of tort has a special branch reserved to address the potential liability of those persons who control premises in relation to other people who enter them. This branch of law is called 'occupier's liability'. Essentially,

> ## an occupier of premises has a duty to take care that in all circumstances, a person who is on the premises with the occupier's knowledge or consent will be reasonably safe.

A customer who can prove that he suffered injury on the shop premises as a result of the retailer's negligence will probably succeed in a legal action against the retailer in a claim for damages as compensation.

Practical Steps to Take to Avoid or Minimise Legal Liability

1. Ensure that all displays are carefully arranged and avoid overloading the shelves.

Neat display shelves not only promote sales, but also reduce the occurrence of accidents (courtesy of the Robinsons Group of Stores).

2. All floor staff should be trained and regularly reminded to be vigilant and alert to any signs of danger and to take immediate steps to redress potentially dangerous situations.

3. Regularly review public liability insurance coverage to ensure, given the level of risk posed by the nature of the business, that the coverage is always realistic and sufficient.

By Patricia Moreira, Lecturer, School of Business, Singapore Polytechnic

RETAIL OPERATIONS

No More Worries with 3 years extended warranty!

Sales Policy

The sales policies of a retail shop aim to reinforce an understanding in the minds of customers before, during and after the sale. They state how, in general, sales transactions are to be carried out to avoid any misunderstanding between the customer and the retailer. Such policies should be communicated to all customers through either the sales staff or proper signs. Four important areas will be discussed in this chapter.

Tills and Receipts

The retailer should ensure that all activities at the cashier counter are processed in a timely, accurate and careful manner. Before doing so, the retailer must decide on the form of payment to be accepted at the cashier counter, for example, cash, credit cards, NETS, cash cards, foreign currencies or personal cheques. Next, the retailer must ensure that the staff are competent in processing these various forms of payment.

A sample of receipt printout

The retailer must also provide proof of purchase to customers through a receipt that specifies appropriate information such as the shop's address and telephone number, the receipt number, date, price and details of the merchandise purchased, and state the shop's refund and exchange policy.

Merchandise Reservation

If the retailer decides to provide reservation service to enhance customer satisfaction, the policy and procedure for this service should be made known to the staff and the customer. The following should be noted each time a customer makes a reservation:

- The reservation details must be recorded in a book or a reservation slip with carbon copies.

- Policies on how long a reservation will be held and whether a deposit is required should be explained clearly to the customer.

- The slip with the customer's name, contact number and name of the sales staff who served the customer should be attached to the reserved merchandise.

- The reserved merchandise should be kept in a designated area so that all staff know where to retrieve the merchandise when needed.

- Upon confirmation of the reservation, the slip is removed to be followed by the usual sales procedure.

- If the reservation is overdued, telephone and remind the customer of their reservation.

- If the reservation is cancelled, the slip is destroyed and the merchandise is put up for sale again.

A sample of a reservation receipt can be found on page 176.

▬ Refund and Exchange

Modern retailers are encouraged to adopt a liberal refund-and-exchange policy. Thus if a customer wishes to return an item, the adjustment should be made promptly. A retail shop's policy on returned items may require that the returned item be accompanied by a sales slip or a price tag, and that the return be made within a defined number of days after the purchase. This requirement must be reflected clearly on the receipt, signs in the shop or be highlighted by the sales staff. However, if the retailer decides not to offer such a service, it must be communicated clearly through the same means to the customers.

Many adjustments for returns are made in cash or a credit slip that can be applied to other purchases within a certain time period. If the returned item was purchased on credit, then the adjustment would consist of crediting the amount back to the account.

The Shop's Name
Address and Telephone Number

CUSTOMER RESERVATION FORM

No. 0001

Date: _____

Name   : _____

Address   : _____

Contact No. : _____

Qty	Description	Unit Price	Amount

*A cash deposit of 20% is required.   Total

*Deposit

Balance

Type of Sales

☐ Cash   ☐ Cheque   ☐ Credit Card No. _____

☐ VIP   ☐ Staff Purchase

I, the undersigned, confirm the sale and agree with the terms and conditions stipulated herein and overleaf.

_____
Signature of Customer

Remarks	Attended by

A sample reservation receipt

The retailer should also establish policies and procedures for merchandise exchange. Sometimes a customer may ask for the replacement of an item with another of the same item, or exchange it for a different item of the same value or a different value. Whatever the reason, the sales staff must be competent in processing such requests efficiently.

Any customer refund or exchange should be recorded in the shop's customer return form, which usually consists of two copies, one for the shop's record and the other to be given to the customer.

An example of a customer return form is shown as follows.

The Shop's Name Address and Telephone Number	

CUSTOMER RETURN FORM

No. 0001

Date: _____

Name   : _____

Address   : _____

Contact No. : _____

Item No.	Qty	Description	Amount

☐ Cash Refund   ☐ Exchange   ☐ Credit Card

Card No. _____

Reasons for Exchange/Refund

Remarks

Issued by   Customer Acknowledgement

Date   Date

Delivery

The delivery policy varies among shops and it also depends on the type of shop. A shop may adopt any of the following:

- No delivery service provided
- Free delivery service for all purchases
- Fee charged for all deliveries
- Free delivery service available only for purchases above a specified minimum amount and a fee charged for purchases below the minimum amount
- Free delivery service available only within the neighbourhood and a fee charged for other destinations

Any delivery should be recorded on the shop's sales memo or invoice, which usually consists of two copies, one for the shop's record and the other to be given to the customer.

The procedures are as follows:

1. The customer is to fill in his/her particulars which include name, contact number and address to which the merchandise is to be delivered.

2. Fix the date and time of delivery by referring to the delivery plan.

"Madam, here's your purchase."

I need help...

Can you show me a Sample Store Policy?

OUR COMMITMENT TO CUSTOMERS

1. **Prices**

   All prices are listed in Singapore dollars and are inclusive of 7% GST.

2. **Payment Mode**

   We accept payment by cash, NETS and VISA only.

3. **Delivery**

   We provide free delivery on purchases of S$100 and above. Delivery will be made within three working days and must be within the main island of Singapore. A delivery charge of S$10 is applicable per delivery for purchases not exceeding S$100. We will contact you to confirm delivery details and delivery times before we send the purchases to you.

4. **Return and Exchange**

   Customers can return or exchange unused, unwashed and unaltered merchandise within 30 days from the date of purchase.

With a receipt: Returned items are refunded at the original purchase price, plus applicable GST, in original method of payment.

Without a receipt: Returned items are refunded at the lowest 'on sale' price within the last 30 days, plus applicable GST, only in the form of a gift voucher.

Exception to our return policy: Discounted merchandise must be returned within seven days of purchase with the original sales receipt.

5. **Reservation**

We can reserve regular items for you for up to three days. However, sales and promotional merchandise cannot be reserved.

6. **Warranties**

All items are supplied with the manufacturer's standard warranty, if any. No other warranties are expressed or implied. We cannot be held liable for the performance of any product, manufacturer or carrier.

Customer Service Decisions

10

Customer service is a set of activities that retailers provide to make the shopping experience more rewarding for customers. These activities not only increase the value the customers receive from the merchandise or services, but also generate positive word-of-mouth communication which attracts new customers.

Goods + Services = Price

Customer service, if used strategically, can provide a competitive advantage to the shop and enhance the retail offering. The extent of customer service to which a retailer provides is determined by:

- The retailer's objectives
- The type of merchandise
- The customers

— A Service Strategy

In Chapter 2, we discussed the importance of customer service. We can conclude that customer service is a process of creating and sustaining customer loyalty. The end objective is to increase customer value and, at the same time, reduce the cost of selling.

Better service does not imply more costly service.

In fact, better service will generate savings as processes are streamlined and as the number of complaints, investigations and rework decrease. Thus many retailers are focusing on customer service as their competitive differentiator.

However, creating and sustaining a corporate culture of service excellence is not easy. Service excellence is more than just smiling employees who make eye contact with their customers. Service excellence is about making, enabling and keeping promises with customers.

In order to achieve consistency and deliver promises through excellent people and practices, a service strategy is required.

A service strategy creates a vision of service excellence for the company.

It helps to clarify service standards to the employees, focus their effort in a common direction, provide a guide for decision-making and build a service culture within the company. It also guides the human resource personnel in hiring the right people.

Developing a service strategy requires the effort and involvement of a team of company leaders and employees. While the managers need to have a clear view of the big picture, the commitment of staff is also important in order for any service initiative to be successful.

Services have to be designed to suit the customers and not the employees. A service strategy should help to differentiate the company from its competitors. Start with a service audit to determine what is important to customers when they visit your retail store. Ask them to envision an ideal retail store. Analyse how your store and your competitors measure up to that standard. Specific standards have to be set for each customer service process, for example, a 24-hour turnaround on customer complaints or inquiries.

Once a service strategy is developed, existing policies, procedures and practices must be aligned to support the implementation of the new strategy. To overcome employee scepticism and foster support, visible service symbols such as a service excellence mission statement, service incentives and measurements must be explained and communicated to all levels of employees.

The Planet Traveller: Travel tips (courtesy of Kingsmen Creatives Ltd)

Equip employees with the skills
to deliver service promises
through training and meetings.

A successful service strategy does not end upon implementation. It requires constant monitoring and review. These include assessing employee performance against service standards and rewarding service excellence; comparing your company's financial performance after the implementation of the service strategy; and benchmarking your services against international best practices. Once you are in control of the system, you should introduce 'service innovation' where necessary. Service innovation means to update your service standards in response to market trends or enhance your service offerings to make competitors irrelevant.

Customer Service Programme

A good customer service programme should consider:

- The types of service objectives: A clearly defined set of service objectives that guides the retailer's efforts on service features and actions

- The features of the service: The types of services provided

- The quality of the service: How the service features are performed

Here are some examples:

Objectives	<ul><li>To create a competitive edge</li><li>To create a specific demand</li><li>To create a strong store image</li><li>To generate store traffic</li><li>To increase customer convenience</li><li>To provide a safe environment</li></ul>
Features	<ul><li>Alteration and repairs</li><li>Complaint resolution</li><li>Delivery and installation</li><li>Guarantee and warranty</li><li>Opening hours</li><li>Payment facilities</li><li>Product information</li><li>Returns and adjustments</li><li>Wrapping and packaging</li></ul>
Quality	<ul><li>Approachability</li><li>Competence</li><li>Convenience</li><li>Courtesy</li><li>Credibility</li><li>Reliability</li><li>Responsiveness</li><li>Security</li></ul>

Lancome: Waiting area to enhance customer service
(courtesy of Kingsmen Creatives Ltd)

Handling Customers Effectively

Customers have the right to:

- Browse the merchandise at their own pace

- Expect quality and reliability in the merchandise purchased

- Expect accurate and relevant merchandise information to be communicated

- Expect assistance in making a purchase

All sales staff should take note of the following attributes for good customer relations:

- Be courteous

- Be enthusiastic

- Always smile

- Be attentive

- Show concern

- Ask the right questions

- Make an extra effort

- Handle purchases with respect

- Be prepared

- Be well informed

- Be positive in problem solving

- Build customer confidence

Inform your customers of any existing credit card promotions

Handling Inquiries

Customers may make inquiries on a number of issues that may be merchandise-related or service-related. A customer record book can be used to keep track of such inquiries and enable follow-up.

The key points to note are:

- Always answer an inquiry with a smile

- Always be polite

- Stop what you are doing and answer the customers' queries patiently

- Never reply with statements such as, "I don't know", or "It's all there".

By answering the customer inquiries in a correct and polite manner, you would have made a good impression on the customer on behalf of the company.

Product Knowledge

Retailers must pick up basic product knowledge to answer customer's queries. Having up-to-date product knowledge is important to being a successful salesperson as it gives customers confidence in the shop and the assurance that the merchandise is suitable in meeting their needs.

Some basic product knowledge include:

- The uses

- The benefits

- The performance

- The material

- The care

- The appearance

- The background

Brochures on product information (courtesy of The Executive Home Store – XZQT)

Handling Complaints

All retailers must have standard policies for handling problems. Such policies must be communicated to all employees. If a rectifiable problem is identified, such as a defective product, the retailer should make restitution on the spot and apologise for the inconvenience caused to the customer. The retailer should offer either a replacement, a credit towards future purchase or a cash refund. Minor complaints may be handled by the sales assistants but customers will often appreciate the attention of their superior.

Service Recovery

In cases where the cause of the problem is difficult to identify; is uncorrectable; or is the result of the customer's unusual request, appropriate steps in effective service recovery may include:

- Listening to the customer
- Providing a fair solution
- Resolving the problem quickly

I need help...

What are some Simple Actions that make Significant Payoffs?

Customers make a purchase based on what they see (e.g. merchandise, store layout), what they hear (e.g. product knowledge, suggestive selling) and what you focus on (e.g. your promotional efforts).

Great customer service inspires loyalty and provides the means to build your average sales, improve profits and retain customers. However, it requires a 100 percent delivery on your promises.

The following questions and answers should help you and your team turn those demanding customers into loyal advocates for your business.

Q: What do your customers want from you?

Availability	... To be ready to help them
Attentiveness	... To listen to their needs and pay attention to details
Courtesy	... To treat them with honour and respect
Credibility	... To speak with conviction on matters that concern them
Efficiency	... To attend to their needs without delay

Empathy	...	To show genuine understanding of their problem
Personal service	...	To offer unique and personalised treatment to solve their problem
Reliability	...	To have consistent performance every day
Trustworthiness	...	To have their best interests at heart

Q: What does excellent customer service include?

- *Attitude*

  Attitude refers to the behaviour that shows that you like to help people and do what you should do. Attitudes are contagious. Since you choose to be in retailing, you should do your very best in what you do, be positive and make each moment a special moment for you, your colleagues and your customers.

- *Actions*

  Actions include face-to-face and telephone communications. Especially important is to watch your body language when you engage in face-to-face communication and watch your tone of voice when you engage in a telephone communication.

- *Excellence*

  Excellence means how well you handle the situation when things go wrong and doing what it takes to satisfy customers' needs without them asking for it.

Q: Dealing with ever demanding customers — Do the old ways work?

Every customer service transaction generally progresses through four steps:

1. Greet (to acknowledge)

2. Listen (to questions and responses)

3. Evaluate (needs)

4. Respond (with an appropriate service)

Each step requires good people skills because you want your customer to walk out of your shop feeling good about the product purchased and service received.

Under normal conditions, customer service requires:

- Good communication skills

- Good understanding of consumer behaviour

- Real desire to provide service to customers

However, difficult conditions are the true test of your customer service skills. Here are some scenarios:

What would you do when:

1. All your customers seem to need your attention at once?

2. Your company makes a mistake and you have an unhappy customer?

3. You encounter an unreasonable customer?

Of course, you should do the best that you can and make the best of a bad situation. Here are some suggestions:

- In an overly busy situation, you should:
  - Be fair
  - Prioritise
  - Give full attention to the customer that you are serving but, at the same time, acknowledge those customers to whom you cannot provide the necessary service immediately

- Handling an unhappy customer requires patience, sensitivity and tact. You should:
  - Listen attentively
  - Verbalise your understanding of the complaint or problem
  - Offer a direct and sincere apology if your company has made a mistake
  - Suggest a solution or ask the customer how he would like to see the problem resolved if there is no solution

By acknowledging your customer's problem and sympathising with him, you have established yourself as someone who wants to help.

- In situations where you encounter an unreasonable customer, you should:
  - Maintain poise
  - Express regrets for any inconvenience caused
  - Stand by your company policy

Do not get angry, do not bring up other issues and do not argue. Seek your superior's assistance to handle the situation if necessary.

Remember:

* It costs more to get a new customer than it does to keep a current one.

* To apologise is to show that you are sorry for the inconvenience caused and not an admission of guilt.

* Customer service begins with the corporate culture and commitment to providing good customer service.

* Companies that offer a variety of services but lacks good customer service will have a difficult time growing their businesses.

The Art of Retail Selling

A retailer meets many customers at the store every day. Once the customers are inside the store, personal selling becomes all important.

Selling is the process of assisting a customer make a decision to buy a product or service. It helps the customer to identify the need or want for the product or service and to understand its features and benefits. Selling requires a lot of time, energy and cost but the payoff can be tremendous. It is, therefore, beneficial for retailers to be aware of effective retail selling approaches so that they can become more confident and professional in selling their products and services to customers.

▬ The Retail Selling Process

Whether selling apparels shoes, furniture or electronic devices, retail salespersons assist customers in finding what they are looking for and try to interest them in buying the merchandise. They describe a product's feature, demonstrate its use or show various models and colours. All these actions that may ultimately lead to a sales transaction form the retail selling process.

The retail selling process consists of eight steps, none of which is less important than any other if the process is to be effective.

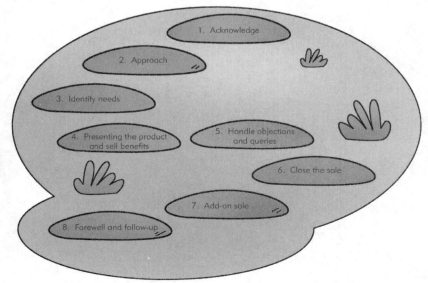

Pre-Customer Contact

In order to effectively handle all the steps in the selling process, the retail salesperson must first be equipped with knowledge, particularly specific knowledge. Such knowledge will help them handle customer inquiries, supply information and overcome objections more confidently.

Here is a list of basic information that the retail salesperson should be equipped with.

Company	
	• The organisation structure • The policies, procedures and rules • The contacts of key personnel • The head office's address and telephone number • Other outlets' addresses, telephone numbers and opening hours • Marketing brochures and advertisements • The operation guidelines of various store equipment (e.g. the cash register)
Product	
	• Reputation of the brand • Country of manufacture • Country of origin • Selling price • When it was released • Prime features and benefits • Quantity available (e.g. limited edition, limited quantity, exclusive, etc.) • How well it is selling • Is there any customer's testimonial • Availability of spare parts • Availability of support services • The duration of the warranty • Storage requirements • Any safety factors to note • Care and maintenance required • Any accessories available

Customers	• Key buying influences
	• How they purchase
	• Frequency of purchase
Competitors	• Product range
	• Features and benefits of their products
	• Selling price
	• Warranty policies
	• Sales promotions
Market	• Industry trends

To most retail salespersons, the greatest challenge of the job is to know enough about the products they sell. This is because things are constantly changing, for example, new models, new releases, etc.

How do the retail salespersons obtain the product information? They can read the product manual (if there is), read about the new releases in magazines, try it out themselves, ask suppliers or ask their colleagues.

The pursuit of knowledge must be a continual process. One can never rest on what was learnt at the last training session. They must stay knowledgeable by keeping abreast with trends, innovations and general market conditions.

The successful application of knowledge, effective selling skills and techniques, and having the proper attitude would help the salesperson to make more sales.

 **Step 1: Acknowledge**

A first impression is hard to change. Thus it is important to create a positive first impression with customers. A simple way to acknowledge the customers' presence and make them feel welcome is by greeting them the moment they enter the store.

Common greetings include:

If the customer is a regular customer of the store, greet the customer by his name, for example, "Welcome, Mr Lee."

Be mindful of the words, tone of voice, facial expression and gesture. All these will communicate to the customer the sincerity and willingness to serve. For example, a lively tone of voice and a sincere smile demonstrate a confident and friendly greeting.

If the salesperson is busy with another customer, he should tell the waiting customer, "I'll be with you in a moment." Such actions will reduce the number of customers who will leave without being served.

When the salesperson is free to help the waiting customer, the initial greeting should be, "Thank you for waiting."

A courteous, creative
     initial contact with the customer
can go a long way
          to promote sales.

However, a greeting need not always be verbal. An acceptable greeting when you are busy serving another customer can be a nod, a smile or just eye contact. This action allows customers to know that you are aware of their presence.

Many customers find it threatening if you march up to them immediately after greeting them. Unless the customer walks straight to you to ask for help, allow the customer a few seconds to 'settle in' before you approach the customer.

However, there are occasions when the salesperson acknowledges and approaches the customer at the same time. This practice is also acceptable.

 Step 2: Approach

Most initial approaches begin in this manner:

Retail salesperson: "Can I help you?"

Many customers are used to hearing this statement and thus the response is usually given without thinking:

Customer: "No, thank you. I'm just browsing."

> ### The most effective way to close a sale is to open it on a positive note.

So, instead of immediately approaching the customer, observe the customer to pick up some clues before starting conversation. By observing, you will probably use one of the following approaches to begin a conversation:

- Social approach
- Product approach
- Service approach

Social Approach

The social approach is recommended when the customer browses and does not show any particular interest in any merchandise. The social approach can be as follows:

- "Good morning, how are you today?"
- "What brings you in on such a gorgeous day?"

The purpose of the above approach is to establish an atmosphere of friendliness to begin a positive connection. Thus you should always use a smile and a pleasant tone of voice.

Open a sale on a positive note

Product Approach

The product approach is recommended when the customer touches a product, tries it out or begins reading the product information on the packaging. The product approach can be as follows:

Customer: "Um, nice lotion."

Retail salesperson: "That's our most popular line. Try it!"

If a customer sits on a sofa to test it out, your opening statement could be:

Retail salesperson: "This is our new arrival. Do you like it?"

Remember, your comments should be a general comment about the product. You can comment on the colour, the uniqueness, the design, the price (if there is a promotion), the brand name, etc.

By using the product approach, you are trying to create an opening conversation with your customer to understand what he wants. Once the customer senses that you are sincerely interested in his needs, the conversation will continue.

Service Approach

The service approach is recommended when the customer knows exactly what he wants, is in a hurry or has a product in his hands. The service approach can be as follows:

- "How can I help you today?"
- "Is there something you are looking for?"
- "Can I help you to bring this item to the cashier counter?"

Combined Approach

Sometimes, the acknowledgement step can be combined with any of the approaches above, for example:

- "Good morning, Mr Chan! How are you today?" (greet and social)
- "Good morning, Ms Ong! We have lots of new arrivals today." (greet and product)
- "Good morning, Mrs Wong! How may I help you today?" (greet and service)

If, despite using the above approaches, the customers say that they are just browsing, do reply by saying:

- "Just let me know if you need any assistance."

Sometimes, you are not sure whether the customer has been approached by your colleagues because you just came out from the store room. In this case, you need only to acknowledge the customer with a friendly greeting first. If possible, check with your colleagues if the customer has been approached.

Step 3: Identify Needs

There are many reasons why a customer buys a product. Whatever the underlying reason is, all customers would want to receive more value from the product they have purchased than what they have paid.

Selling the way the customer wants to buy is more important than selling the way the retailer likes to sell.

To assist the customer in receiving more value from the product they purchase, the retail salesperson should use consultative selling, that is, focus on the customers' needs and then provide product or products that meet those needs. In other words, instead of product features and benefits, the salesperson should emphasise the customers and their goals.

Talk to Your Customers

The primary aim of speaking to customers is to find out as much about their needs as possible. These include:

- Purpose of buying
- Price range
- Personal preference
- Product features or specifications

"How do I identify customers' needs?"

Knowing the needs and wants of customers will help build a picture of what you can do for them. This will, in turn, open new opportunities for sales. For example:

- By knowing the purpose of buying a product (i.e. what the product is used for), the sales associate is able to make an appropriate recommendation or an alternative if the product wanted by the customer is not available.

- By knowing the price or price range that the customer is willing to pay for a product, the sales associate is able to suggest something within the customer's budget.

- By knowing the customer's preference, the sales associate is able to know the customer's likes and dislikes.

It is important to note that what is popular with most people may not be what the customer like.

- By knowing the product features or specifications that the customer wants, the sales person is able to help the customer find a suitable product.

Listen, Observe and Ask

When the retail salesperson communicates with a customer to identify needs, bear in mind the following:

- **Learn to listen**

  Being attentive to the customer's needs makes the customer feel important.

The best salespeople are those who listen more than they talk.

The retail sales associate should ask reflective questions (where necessary) to show that he is listening and to clarify what is being heard. For example, "Since you mentioned that you will be travelling a lot, would you then prefer to buy a more durable suitcase?"

By listening, the salesperson is able to pick up information that can help to make a sale. By listening attentively, the salesperson need not ask too many questions. Asking too many questions can make the customer feel that the salesperson does not want to show him too many products.

- Observe body language

Body language (or non-verbal communication) is an important part of communication which, according to at least one study, constitutes more than 50 percent of what we are communicating. Body language refers to the use of body movements as a form of communication. For example, if the customer keeps looking at the watch while talking to the salesperson, it can imply that the customer is in a hurry. But the salesperson must be careful not to draw a wrong conclusion. It will be good to ask the customer, "Are you in a hurry?"

The retail salesperson should also use appropriate body language when listening to his/her customers. These include nodding, maintaining eye contact or smiling.

- Ask the right questions

Questions that have a "Yes" or "No" answer are called closed questions. For example, asking the customer if they would like a product with more benefits at a special price is unlikely to get a negative response. A positive response will usually generate a customer's interest in the product.

Always start with questions that can only be answered "Yes" or "No".

Closed questions also help to clarify information. But, do not use too many closed questions as it can make the customer feel like he is going through an interrogation.

- Ask open-ended questions

The best salesperson is one who moves on to asking open-ended questions after asking the right questions. This will reveal more about the customer's needs. Open-ended questions usually begin with *What, When, Why, Who, Where* and *How*.

For example:

- "What colour do you have in mind?"
- "When do you intend to wear the dress?"
- "Where is the party being held?"
- "How do you like to dress for that party?"

But bear in mind not to ask too many questions.

Keep the questions simple. Also, a good mix of open and closed questions can be helpful in gathering information about the customer's needs and wants, and match them to the appropriate product that the store sells.

- **Ask the customer if he has other queries**

   Seek to clarify the customer's doubts. If the customer's further queries are questions such as "Do you have a new piece in stock?" or "When can you deliver?", these are cues for you to close the sale.

In addition to the above, the retail salesperson must also be aware of some factors that influence the buying decisions of customers. One such important factor is cultural influence.

Culture affects a person's actions and decisions.

It includes customs, values and beliefs. For example, if you are serving an Indian customer who is looking for a leather bag, do not show this customer a bag that is made of cow skin. This is because many Indians are Hindus, and Hindus consider the cow as a sacred animal. Thus such a bag is a taboo item for the Indian customer.

Step 4: Present the Products and Sell Benefits

After identifying the customer's needs, the retail salesperson is ready to present and sell the merchandise to the customer. The optimal use of product knowledge is very important in presenting the merchandise to the customer.

Present the Product

Involve the customer

The best way to present a product is to involve the customer. Product knowledge can be used to get customer involvement. For example, show the customer several features of a product and then have the customer try it. Always allow the customer to touch and feel the product.

Limit the choices

Based on the needs of the customers select a few products (usually not more than three) for the customer to consider or try.

> ## Limited choices can often help to promote sales.

Giving the customer too many choices can cause indecisiveness and thus the purchase will most likely be postponed.

Sell enthusiastically

In presenting the merchandise to the customer, the salesperson must be enthusiastic about the product.

For example:

- Bring the product out of the cabinet and let the customer have a closer look.

- Demonstrate the product in such a way that it captures attention and is easy to use.

Do not bore the customer with too many facts, especially those that the customer already knows. If the needs have been identified through earlier conversations with the customer, the salesperson just needs to

emphasise the facts that meet those needs and highlight other interesting features and benefits that may enhance the sale of the product.

If the customer is keen to know more, then the salesperson can proceed to explain further.

Sell Benefits

So, what makes the customer buy? Benefits!

Every product has features. A feature is a characteristic of a product. It is tangible. It also includes the brand, price or material. These information is usually shown on the product packaging.

A feature offers benefits, that is, a solution to a specific need. Benefits mean what the product can do for customers. Rather than simply describing its features,

Highlighting the product's benefits is more likely to result in a sale.

Successful selling requires the salesperson to show customers how the product meets their needs.

For example, a customer may not be as concerned about how much horsepower (a feature) a lawnmower has as much as he is interested in how fast (a benefit) the lawnmower can cut grass.

Remember...

features tell
but benefits sell!

In selling benefits, the retail salesperson must always put himself in the customer's shoes. Always look at the product as a solution and understand what issues it can address. This will indirectly help the salesperson to illustrate how the product's benefits can meet the customer's needs or solve the customer's problem.

There are, however, two types of benefits: rational benefits and emotional benefits. Rational benefits offer solutions (a need) to the customer's problem. Emotional benefits appeal to the good feelings (a want) of the customer. For example, a particular brand of watch has good quality and is trendy. In this case, brand is a feature, good quality is a rational benefit and trendy is an emotional benefit.

How Can Selling Be Enhanced?

Selling can be enhanced if the retail salesperson can

quantify
the benefits.

For example, the number of testimonials from customers who have used the product and are very satisfied with the product can be used to quantify the benefits.

Another example is to equate the benefit's in terms of dollars and cents to the cost of the product. If the retail salesperson can prove that a product has saved a customer $500 on electrical bills over one year, and it only costs $100 to buy the product, then the customer is more likely to buy the product.

In addition, it will be helpful if the salesperson can differentiate a product from its competitors. The retail salesperson should always be prepared to answer this question from the customer: "Why should I buy this product from you?" or "Why should I buy this brand?" If the salesperson has at least two or three reasons for these questions, particularly based on quantifiable benefits the product offers, then there is a high chance that the product will be sold.

It is important that the
salesperson should
never 'run down' one product
to promote another.

Instead, he should point out the extra value of the alternative. The salesperson's role is to ensure the customer is aware of the options available and the benefits of each. For example:

DON'T SAY

SAY

Step 5: Handle Objections and Queries

Very often, the customer may express some concerns about the merchandise or question the need for it. These doubts and concerns are called objections or queries. Objections are reasons that customers have for not buying the merchandise. Queries are questions raised because customers do not have enough information about the merchandise. Thus objections and queries are related. If a customer's query about the features of the merchandise is not handled properly, it would lead to an objection to buy it.

Generally, most retail salespeople are afraid of objections. Objections are a natural part of the selling process. They do not mean that the sale is lost. In fact,

the presence of objections implies opportunities to close a sale.

In most cases, to overcome an objection, the retail salesperson needs only to do more selling.

Reasons for Objections

Customers raise objections because

- They are doubtful of the information given by the retail salesperson about the merchandise.

- They do not have enough information about the merchandise to make a rational decision.

- They are doubtful about whether the merchandise will meet their needs.

- They do not find the price of the merchandise value for money.

A customer's objections are reasons for not buying the merchandise.

Guidelines to Overcome Objections

Generally to overcome objections, the retail salesperson needs to:

Action	Example
Listen and acknowledge	"This is a good point. I should have explained it to you earlier."
Ask questions to understand	"What are important features to you?"
Empathise with the customer	"Yes, I do agree with you but this item can help you save a lot in terms of energy consumption in the long run."

Types of Objections

Objections could be met by the salesperson in several ways.

Types of Objection	Ways to Overcome objection

Product

Characteristic
Related to the suitability of the product such as style, colour, size, materials, etc.

- Restate the features and benefits.
- If the objection is valid, stress other benefits of the product.
- If the objection is invalid, provide the customer with the correct information.

If the blouse really looks good on the customer and there isn't any other colours:

This blouse looks good but the colour is not what I wanted.

Yes, it's true this is not the colour you wanted but the style suits you very well. Also, such colour will not go out of fashion. The price is also very value for money.

- If possible, provide some photos to show how the blouse and colour can mix and match with others.

Time

Characteristic
Concerned about whether it is the right time to buy the product now

- If there are benefits to buy now, inform the customer about the benefits.

- If there are no real benefits to buy now, reassure the customer about the product or give the customer some time to think about it by offering to reserve the item for him.

Price

Characteristic

Related to value for money and whether there is a possibility of getting the item cheaper elsewhere

- If the customer can afford the merchandise, stress the benefits to raise the perceived value of the product.

- If the customer mentions budget constraint's, recommend a close alternative that is less expensive to meet the customer's needs.

Service

Characteristic
Concerned about the services offered by the retailer

- If possible provide alternatives.
- If not possible stress other benefits.

If the customer does not drive:

Would you like to leave these merchandise with us first until you have finished your shopping? We can then help you to bring them to the taxi.

I wish your store offers delivery service.

OR

OR

I am sorry we do not offer delivery service but the price is really attractive and you may not be able to get such a price elsewhere.

If the customer drives:

Can I help you take all these merchandise to your car?

Need

Characteristic

Concerned about whether there is a need for the product

- Stress the product's benefits
- Provide reassurance

Store

Characteristic

Concerned with the store image and merchandise variety

- Establish relationship
- Encourage visit

Step 6: Close the Sale

Closing the sale is a very important step. Very often, sales are lost because the retail salesperson fails to close the sale promptly. The retail salesperson either closes the sale too early or misses the buying signals to close the sale.

Buying Signals

A buying signal is something the customer says (verbal) or does (non-verbal) that would indicate that he is ready to buy. Here are some common buying signals

- The customer asks questions about the benefits that the salesperson has mentioned earlier.

- The customer prefers one merchandise over the others after a few products have been presented to him.

- Customer seeks the opinion of his friend or partner who is shopping with him; customer calls over his partner or friend whom he is shopping with to look at the product.

- The customer asks whether he can pay by credit card.

- The customer asks whether there is any discount or free gift.

- The customer tries on a product (e.g. a watch) and seems interested to keep it on.

- The customer keeps looking at a product with serious interest.

- The customer keeps taking up the product.

Once the customer has given a buying signal, the salesperson should stop selling and try to close the sale.

Ways to Close a Sale

Here are some closing techniques.

Closing technique	Example
Ask for the sale	" Can I wrap this item for you now?"
Ask questions	" This watch is unique and really looks good on you, doesn't it?"
Stress benefits	" This book is really a good buy. It is comprehensive and easy to read."
Offer a service	" Can I arrange for the item to be delivered to your house this afternoon?"
Give a choice	" Do you want the sofa in white or black?"
Offer an incentive	" If you buy now, you will get an additional 10 percent off the already discounted price."
Better not wait	" If you want this camera, you should consider buying it now. In fact, this is our last piece in stock."

- It is important to note that if this technique is used to make a sale, the salesperson has to be honest. If the customer buys, then returns to the store the next day and sees that the store does have another one, the salesperson could lose this customer.

Closing technique	Example
If I can... will you...	" If I can bring forward the delivery date, will you place your order now?"
Offer to place a special order	" We do not carry that model but if you are interested, we can specially place an order for you."

After all objections have been met, the retail salesperson should allow the customer time to decide. If the customer says yes, proceed to process the payment. If the customer says no, accept his decision. However, let the customer know that he is always welcome to call upon you again if he or she needs further information.

It is important for the retail salesperson to note that putting pressure on customers to buy may boost sales but he may risk making the customers feel unhappy with their purchase. This could make customers less likely to come to the store again. They may even return the products when they have had time to think things over more carefully.

Thus the retail salesperson must try to establish a continuing relationship with all the customers instead of just concentrating on making sales.

— Step 7: Add-On Sale

After the customer has made a purchase, the salesperson can make a suggestion for a possible additional sale, that is, selling add-ons. Also known as suggestion selling, add-on sale is an extra item that is sold with a purchase. Such an action not only adds value to the business, it also adds value to the customer.

In many cases, suggestion selling may help the customer to avoid another shopping trip to buy that needed item that they had not thought about.

Suggesting additional purchase with purchase is value-adding to both the retailer and the customer.

Good suggestion selling makes sales and builds confidence in the company's business.

In fact, most customers like to receive valid suggestions.

There are two types of add-on sellings – related merchandise and unrelated merchandise.

Related merchandise is usually accessories for or complements to the product that the customer has purchased.

Examples of selling related merchandise:

• When the customer buys a shirt, what about a tie to go with it?

• If a torch is purchased, what about the batteries to turn it on?

• If a suit is bought, what about a new shirt that goes well with the colour?

Selling unrelated merchandise is a suggestion to the customer especially when there are specials or providing information to the customer when there are new arrivals. This can be done after the customer has made a purchase and is waiting for the payment to be processed.

Examples of selling unrelated merchandise:

• When the customer buys a bottle of shampoo (normal size), inform him that it also comes in jumbo economy size.

• When the customer buys a lipstick, inform her that there is a new batch of facial masks that just arrived.

If possible, the salesperson should get the suggested item, show it to the customer and explain the reason for such a suggestion. The salesperson should also take the initiative to offer additional service where possible. For example, if a person brings in a watch to be repaired, ask the customer whether he would like the watch to be cleaned while it is taken apart. This type of initiative shows how much the retailer cares about the customer and usually results in more repeat business.

However, the following are not good examples of suggestion selling because there are no products being recommended:

- "Is there anything else you need?"

- "Do you need me to get you something else?"

Selling Up

Add-on sale can sometimes involve selling up, that is, selling a product which is of higher value. The retail salesperson should consider taking this selling approach if:

- There are extra benefits with the higher-value product.

- The quality of the higher-value product is more value for money.

- The performance of the higher-value product is better.

However, the salesperson should not force or trick the customer into buying the more expensive product. The focus should be on the customer's needs.

Step 8: Farewell and Follow-Up

Even after the salesperson has successfully closed a sale, there are still things to be done. Completing the transaction includes handing a receipt to the customer, packaging the merchandise appropriately and asking whether the customer needs further assistance.

Farewell

The closing statements, "Thank you for shopping at ..." and "Have a nice day", are commonly used after the customer has paid for the merchandise and is about to leave the store. This closing statement is a form of sales follow-up. If done with enthusiasm, it allows the customer to leave on a positive note, thereby increasing the chances of repeat business by the customer.

In some situations, the retail salesperson should offer the customer a business card (if there is one) or the store information card. This happens if the customer is still considering the product and wants a day or two to make a decision. The card will serve as a reminder that if the customer decides to buy, the salesperson will be ready to serve.

Follow-Up

Follow-up is a part of every sale. Follow-up may also involve checking on any promises that were made to the customer after the sale.

For example, if a delivery is supposed to take place on Friday, the salesperson should check to make sure that the promise is met. If the promise is not met, notify the customer of the problem promptly. Good sales follow-up will avoid any inconvenience caused to the customer, for example, having the customer wait for the delivery or call to ask about the delivery on that day.

In another instance, the customer will certainly be pleased if the carpet cleaning service company telephones the customer the next day after cleaning his carpets to check that everything is satisfactory.

A business with a reputation for sales follow-up is going to obtain additional business because it shows that the company does care for the customer even after the sale.

Sincere sales follow-up
builds goodwill
and encourages
repeat business.

— Get Ready to Sell by Building Confidence

Having confidence in yourself and your product has a direct influence on your ability to sell successfully. A self-confident salesperson is one who speaks clearly and answers questions assuredly.

If you do not have confidence in yourself and do not believe in the product that you sell, your customers could sense it and might not buy from you. This is because your level of self-confidence can show in your behaviour, your body language, how you speak and what you say. Self-confident salespeople inspire confidence in their customers.

Self-confidence comes from a strong belief in yourself and that is something you can learn over time. To help build that confidence, you must have a good understanding of your product, your customers, your competition and the most effective selling techniques.

I need help...

Who is my Greatest Weapon?

Retail is a competitive business. Even if the product you are selling is unique, you will still face competition. There is always another store near you that is also targeting the same customers. The choices of where to spend money are infinite but the customers' disposable income is limited.

In today's competitive and increasingly 'commoditised' market, customers expect a retail selling process that emphasises superior product knowledge or the ability to ask questions. To win sales, many retailers resort to price promotions. However, customers that are gained solely on the basis of price will be lost the next time a competitor hold a sale.

There will always be competitors who lure customers with better prices

To differentiate from other retailers and

to discourage customers buying from other based on price differences,

the retailer must adopt a customer-focused selling process.

This requires the retailer to identify the criteria customers use to evaluate their various alternatives before making a purchase decision. The retailer will then adapt their selling tactics to the different phases of the customer's buying process so as to influence customers early in their decision-making process.

However, this method of selling requires the retailer to take time and effort to build a relationship with the customer and to understand what the customer really needs. When the true value is understood, new and unique means of meeting the need can be developed. Customers want to see action taken to meet their wants and needs. This extra effort will lead to greater profit. This is because customers will not pay for product features and services that they do not value, but they will pay a premium for those that they do.

Competing on the basis of customer relationships is not just about using data mining or customer relationship management applications to gather data to understand your customers.

Building customer relationships requires the effort of all employees in your company.

Customers judge your company or brand by how well they are treated by staff they come in contact with. No matter how creative your advertising is or how persuasive your salespeople are, customers will not stay long if your employees do not take care of them! Your effort to create a favourable impression of your brand or company can be undermined by your employees if you do not take care of the people who take care of your business. Thus you should start to instill customer-focused values as part of your corporate culture through a variety of communication, educational and motivational activities.

Management Commitment

Focusing a company on customers is not just a matter of declaring a new policy. The management needs to be involved and committed to setting goals, modelling behaviour, committing resources, and communicating to all employees for their full support. In addition, the management cannot just start the process and walk away; they have to be continuously involved and set a good example. Employees heed what the managers do, not what they say.

Communication

Communicate to let employees know the company's mission and goals and how they can help contribute to achieving them on an ongoing basis (e.g. staff meetings, internal newsletter, training programmes, etc.), not just during new employee orientation.

Reinforce the importance of their roles in contributing to customer satisfaction even if they may never get to see the customer. They need to believe that they can make a difference whether they are in production, accounting or information support services. If each person in the company aims to satisfy the person he is producing work for, the customer will likely benefit the most. For example, if you manage data processing efficiently in a bank, you will be able to provide information to your colleague, the bank teller, who will be able to give the bank customers the accurate balances they need.

Education/Training

Customer surveys can only indicate how well the company is meeting the goals that they think are important.

The best way to understand customer value is to talk to the customer.

The front-line employees must be trained to ask the right questions so as to gather data to determine customer value.

The information collected must be compiled and internalised. Such information must be regularly shared to help employees serve the customers better.

Educate employees on one another's roles by switching roles. This can help build empathy for each other's job. This, in turn, helps to strengthen employees' relationship and reinforce teamwork.

Make training easy and fun. Get employees involved in the process of measuring service quality. For example, gather a team of employees to critique the service of a particular store. Then let them apply what they have learn to their own store service.

Motivation

Motivation involves more than just displaying motivational posters or customers' letters of appreciation to promote customer focus.

> Involving employees in brainstorming ideas to improve customer satisfaction is also a form of motivation.

It shows that the company listens to and values their feedback.

Other common forms of motivational techniques include:

- Empowerment (e.g. giving employees reasonable power to handle problems)

- A word of praise (e.g. "You did a great job. Well done!")

- Rewards (e.g. promotion, pay increment, performance bonus, travel incentives, etc.)

- Recognition (e.g. appeal to employee's pride through certificate presentation by senior management; recognise the 'service hero' through in-house newsletters or display service awards where everyone can see them).

Competitors can copy
your products and services,

but not the relationship
between your employees and
customers.

Employees are truly your competitive advantage. Communicating with, educating and motivating your employees must be an ongoing process. In a marketplace of low growth, price wars and product commoditisation,

building customer relationship
will lead to customer loyalty,
which can be the key to
continued success and
income growth.

RETAIL OPERATIONS

Merchandise
Decisions

12
CHAPTER

The field of retailing is constantly changing as new product and market opportunities develop. Regardless of the size of the shop, a successful retailer must continue to satisfy his existing customers and attract new customers to strengthen his market position. One of the prime areas of concern, particularly for small retailer, is effective merchandise management.

Major decision-making areas in merchandise management include:

- Sales forecasting and planning

- Merchandise planning

- Merchandise budgeting

- Inventory analysis

- Purchasing activity

- Selling activity

- Merchandise analysis and control

A successful retail operation requires the right types of merchandise assortment, bought at the right time, in the right place, in the right quantity and at the right price. To accomplish this, the retailer has to make decisions on what to buy, how much, from whom and when to buy.

The Five Rights of Merchandising

The Right Type

The type and variety of merchandise offered are major determinants of the business the retailer is in and will have an impact on how the customer perceives the shop.

Thus the retailer must decide on the merchandise policy to be adopted, that is, either specialised (carry a few related product lines) or general (carry a wide range of product lines). Moreover, the quality of merchandise must relate to the target market.

The type of merchandise to stock will also depend on how innovative the retailer wants to be, that is, whether the retailer wants to be a fashion leader or a fashion follower.

A specialised product line (courtesy of Aussino Group Ltd)

The Right Time

It is important to time the arrival of the merchandise to meet daily or seasonal needs. The timing (whether of new or repeat orders) will depend on:

- Accurate sales forecast

- Order and delivery lead time

- Maximum or minimum quantity of stocks required to be held by the retailer at any point in time

The Right Location

There are two aspects to the concept of location. First, if the retailer has more than one outlet, the appropriate merchandise range to be sold at each outlet must be carefully considered. It may not be necessary to sell all the merchandise ranges in all the shops as the size and customers of each shop differ. Some retailers may group their outlets into various sizes before determining the merchandise to be carried by the relevant shops. Second, the location of the merchandise within the shop must also be considered carefully.

A well-located store

The Right Quantity

Once the type of merchandise is determined, the breadth (the number of distinct goods categories) and depth (variety in any one goods category) of assortment must be developed. The breadth and depth comprise the retailer's merchandise-mix. To maximise profitability, it is necessary to optimise both the depth and breadth.

To avoid overstocking, the amount of merchandise ordered must relate to the demand for it. Other considerations include seasonal factors, stockturn and whether the merchandise is a basic item or a fashion one.

It is also important that the retailer identifies and maintains a good stock level of the fast-moving merchandise. Very often, fast-moving merchandise contributes to the major bulk of total sales.

The Right Price

Traditionally, the price of merchandise is determined by the cost of goods plus a certain amount of profit. However, this is no longer the reasonable approach in today's competitive market. Besides sales volume, expenses and price adjustments, the pricing decision is also influenced by:

- Target market (mass or exclusive)
- Competition (analysing the direct competitor's pricing strategy)
- The Company's objectives (the overall strategy the company is adopting)
- Suppliers (increase in prices)
- Financial institutions (adjustments to interest rates, which will affect the cost of goods sold if the business relies on bank loans)
- Government (changes to the legal framework, for example, the Fair Trading Act)

The use of the following pricing tactics is common among retailers:

- Price linings (distinct selling prices)
- Price zones (low-price, mid-price and high-price)
- Odd pricing (for example, $9.90)
- Even pricing (for example, $100)
- Multiple-unit pricing (for example, 1 for $9.90, 2 for $15)

- Complementary pricing (for example, the sale of a shirt and tie)

- Fixed pricing (no bargaining)

- Flexible pricing (allows for negotiation)

A "one-price" store (courtesy of Ricky Lim)

Merchandise Buying

To increase merchandising effectiveness, the retailer cannot be everything to everybody. Regardless of the format or the market segment in which the retailer operates, the retailer has to create a competitive advantage by focusing on its product offerings and narrowing its market concentration. This means that

the retailer has to offer enough
of a selection to satisfy
target customers
and to focus on the
well-defined target market
even as it
expands geographically.

A unique storefront in Metro Town, Vancouver (courtesy of Ricky Lim)

A typical buying process includes the following:

- Review existing merchandise and the sales performance

- Identify new merchandise

- Analyse the market and demand for existing and new merchandise

- Plan for the type, brand and quantity of merchandise needed

- Select the sources of merchandise

- Negotiate for the purchase of merchandise

- Place orders and follow up on the orders placed

- Receive and inspect the merchandise

- Price the merchandise

- Place the merchandise on the selling floor or in the storeroom

- Promote and sell the merchandise

- Review the assortment sales trends every week and identify merchandise performing significantly above or below expectations as 'action items'

- Re-order merchandise that remains in demand

- Use markdowns to get rid of merchandise (clearance) or to generate sales (promotional)

- Return underperforming merchandise to the supplier if the terms of purchase allow

What to Buy

The type of merchandise a retailer wants to sell depends largely on the store's image and the customers he wants to attract. For example, an exclusive boutique that caters to upmarket customers who demand good ambience, personal service and unique merchandise will have to sell merchandise that is expensive, trendy and sophisticated.

However, predicting the customers' needs and wants are not easy. To avoid buying and stocking inappropriate merchandise, the retailer needs various sources of information:

- Past sales information

- Feedback from sales associates

- Customer surveys

- Observation of customer behaviour

- Comparison-shopping at other shops

- Suppliers

- Trade publications

- Trade shows

How Much to Buy

Obviously, it is necessary to have enough stock to accommodate the needs of customers, that is, to have a stock level that is large enough to serve most potential customers. Here are some guidelines on what and how much to buy:

- Carry merchandise that will sell in the shop; do not follow too closely what sells well in the competitor's shop.

- Carry a few brands of styles and price lines that have a constant demand.

- Carry a complete assortment of these brand styles and price lines.

- Do not carry too much unusual merchandise.

- Do not buy excessive quantities because of extra discounts.

- Order only merchandise that is needed, that is, do not place orders across the board (for example, ordering one dozen of an item without checking the details) as this will result in duplication of similar merchandise.

The retailer can use a merchandise plan to determine how much to buy for each month. This plan should be completed in advance and serve as a guide to actual buying. Merchandise planning is usually done on a six-month basis. An example of a typical form for developing a merchandise plan can be found on the next page.

In developing the merchandise plan, it is important to take into consideration the planned activities or events for the various months so that the monthly planned sales are more realistic and achievable, and that sufficient stock is being purchased.

The retailer may also draft an assortment plan to determine how the dollar will be spent for specific merchandise, that is, to plan the variety (width) and assortment (breadth and depth) of an optimum range of merchandise for the shop to meet customers' requirements. The concept of this assortment plan is based on the use of a budget and the allocation of percentages to various categories of merchandise that a retailer wishes to purchase.

For example, a retailer of men's wear wishes to spend S$100,000 on the purchase of men's apparel (tops) to achieve next year's planned sales.

SIX-MONTH MERCHANDISING PLAN

	Each Month	January	February	March	April	May	June	Total
Sales Percent								
Sales	Last year							
	Planned							
	Revision							
	Actual							
+ Inventory (end of month)	Last year							
	Planned							
	Revision							
	Actual							
+ Reductions (markdowns + shortages + discounts)	Last year							
	Planned							
	Revision							
	Actual							
– Inventory (beginning of month)	Last year							
	Planned							
	Revision							
	Actual							
= Purchases (retail price)	Last year							
	Planned							
	Revision							
	Actual							
Remarks								

From past sales records, the retailer noted the following information:

- Career wear accounted for 60 percent of the total sales turnover for men's tops.

- Brand 1 accounted for 50 percent of the total sales turnover for career wear.

- Plain-coloured tops accounted for 70 percent of Brand 1's total sales turnover.

- The S$59 price point of the plain-coloured tops of Brand 1 accounted for 50 percent of that category's sales turnover.

Thus the retailer plans to buy more of such merchandise. Here is an example of a part of the assortment plan.

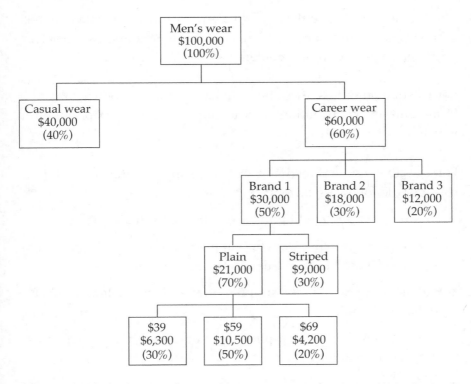

From the above assortment plan, the retailer will buy 162 pieces of shirts (S$6,300 ÷ S$39) to sell at S$39, 178 pieces (S$10,500 ÷ S$59) to sell at S$59, and 61 pieces (S$4,200 ÷ S$69) to sell at S$69 for the whole of next year. This assortment plan can also be used to plan for colours and sizes. The retailer can draft a similar plan for casual wear.

Note that planning is usually done based on retail selling price. The retailer will then negotiate with the supplier for the appropriate cost price based on the type of margin that the retailer wishes to maintain for his shop.

From Whom to Buy

The success of the retail business also depends on the suppliers. The retailer is dependent on a predictable supply of merchandise at competitive prices and with sufficient promotional support.

The retailer can buy either manufacturer's brands or private label brands from domestic or overseas manufacturers, wholesalers, importers, agents or other retailers.

For existing suppliers, the retailer must conduct periodic evaluation to measure the contribution of each supplier at every price point for which he is responsible.

For selecting new or retaining existing suppliers, the retailer may consider the following factors:

- Credit terms: Are credit purchases allowed? What are the terms?

- Distribution policies: Does the supplier limit sales of the particular styles purchased to a well-defined geographic area?

- Exclusive rights: Will the supplier offer exclusive selling rights for some merchandise?

- Information: Will the supplier share any important merchandise data or information?

- Innovativeness: Are the supplier's products innovative or conservative? Do they meet the merchandise policies?

- Investment cost: How large is the total investment cost with the supplier for the selected merchandise?

- **New products:** How frequently does the supplier introduce new lines of merchandise?

- **Order processing time:** How fast will the merchandise ordered be delivered?

- **Price quality:** Which supplier provides the best merchandise at the lowest price?

- **Promotional support:** How supportive is the supplier in offering special products for special events or in offering advertising allowances?

- **Reliability and ethics:** Will the supplier consistently fulfill all promises?

- **Re-orders:** Can the supplier fulfill re-orders promptly?

When to Buy

Generally, not all retailers have the same buying time frame. The policies of each retailer dictate when is the best time to buy. Budget shop retailers, for example, will buy opportunistically; they buy when the suppliers are ready to clear their merchandise at greatly reduced prices.

It is important to note that all merchandise should be bought so that there will be sufficient stock to meet customer demand, taking into consideration the retailer's merchandising policies, sales forecasts, seasonal factors, delivery lead time, quantity discounts and the need to control inventory levels at an acceptable level.

— Merchandise Control

The profitability of a shop depends on how well each merchandise item performs. Thus, the retailer must monitor the profitability of each item and decide whether to keep it in stock or discontinue it.

Here are two ways to analyse merchandise performance:

1. **Compare actual sales with planned sales**

   The retailer should monitor closely the actual sales against planned sales (with the assistance of a computerised POS system) to determine whether more merchandise needs to be ordered or whether the merchandise should be put up for sale. There is no exact rule for determining such actions. The decision depends on experience with the merchandise in the past or whether there are any forthcoming advertising and promotions planned by the retailer or suppliers.

2. **Rank the merchandise**

   All retail businesses need to offer a variety of merchandise to enhance sales. Some items are less profitable but are often important because they either attract customers or complement other items in the shop. For example, batteries may be low-profit/high-volume merchandise but they are necessary for a retailer who sells many battery-operated toys.

The retailers may group and rank the merchandise based on their sales or profit performance and manage their merchandise accordingly. This process can help the retailer determine which items should never be out of stock and which items should be marked down as soon as possible.

For example, an apparel retailer may group and define his shirt department into various categories:

- Category A items as best-selling items
- Category B items as up-and-coming fashion items (for example, new styles or new colours)
- Category C items as test-marketing items
- Category D items as unsaleable or outdated items

Thus, the retailer must:

- Ensure that Category A items, which generally include basic colours and sizes, must never be out of stock.

- Pay close attention to Category B items, which may include other better selling colours or designs.

- Plan to carry category C items only in certain sizes or make special orders to meet stock-out conditions for these items.

- Return (if possible, depending on the purchase terms with the suppliers) or mark down Category D items as soon as possible.

I need help...

How do I Maintain a Healthy Balance between Inventory and Sales?

INVENTORY   SALES

Improve the Timing of Purchases

A retailer can lower inventory without affecting the merchandise selection by timing his purchases. Buying more closely to the demand patterns can improve sales without affecting profitability. This is especially true for seasonal products. The general guideline is not to buy and stock seasonal goods too far in advance of the selling period. The early arrival of new products shortens the selling period for existing products, which may increase the pressure to clear them through markdowns.

Reduce Markdowns

Although markdowns cannot be avoided, a retailer can increase sales by controlling the amount of markdowns. This can be achieved through better advertising, display, in-store promotions and personal selling. Retailers who operate multiple outlets can decrease the need for markdowns by shifting merchandise among the outlets, especially to outlets that can sell more of the merchandise at the regular price.

Control the Depth of the Merchandise

A retailer should identify the optimal inventory levels for each category of merchandise and, at the same time, strike a balance between variety and assortment. Limiting variety or assortment to reduce inventory level may lead to customer disappointment with the merchandise selection and they may stop patronising the shop.

Marketing
Practices

A retailer could stock the most attractive and competitively priced merchandise, and have a convenient location but still fail to attract customers if there is no communication with customers. Retail communication can be accomplished in many ways.

Bus Advertisements (courtesy of Kingsmen Creatives Ltd)

Advertising

Promotional advertising, which focuses on attracting immediate customer traffic and creating sales, is commonly used by most retailers. The common types of media used are newspapers, magazines, posters, flyers and mailers. To preserve customer goodwill, retailers should be careful in selecting the type of merchandise to be advertised.

Merchandise that should be advertised includes the following:

- Merchandise that is distinctive.

- Merchandise that is currently popular.

- Merchandise that is offered at reduced or special prices.

An event advertisement

An advertising slogan

Merchandise that should not be advertised is as follows:

- Merchandise that is leftover stock and offered at regular prices.

- Merchandise that is available in a limited quantity that does not justify the advertising expenses or satisfy the demand for it.

- Merchandise with uncertain in-store date.

- Merchandise that has been advertised previously and does not give any indication of becoming more saleable.

▬ Sales Promotion

Sales promotion comprises promotional activities other than advertising, personal selling and public relations. It is a short-term incentive to encourage a stronger market response and stimulate consumer purchase. It is designed to support other communication activities.

Promotional activities
(courtesy of the Robinsons Group of Stores)

The objective of a sales promotion is to encourage customers passing the retail shop to:

Stop and Browse

↓

Browse and Buy

↓

Buy More

↓

Repeat the Purchase

Retailers can use a variety of sales promotion techniques to attract new customers, meet competition, introduce new merchandise or reduce seasonal decline in sales.

A Christmas promotion (courtesy of Aussino Group Ltd)

For example, to increase sales, the retailer can:

- Increase the number of transactions by using sales promotion methods to attract more people to the shop and also to provide attractive incentives for customers to make purchases

- Increase the size of the average sale by having promotions on merchandise with a high margin and also to offer other incentives to buy more.

Promotional campaign by the Singapore Tourism Board

Sales promotions can originate from either the supplier or the retailers themselves. Here are some examples:

Supplier-Initiated Sales Promotion	Retailer-Initiated Sales Promotion
• In-store activities such as price-off pack, premiums, competitions, sampling, price-off coupons, buy-one get-one-free, multipacks and demonstrators	• Price promotions such as annual sales • In-house discount cards • Free gifts with a certain amount of purchase • Joint promotions with other retailers

Advertising and promotions are great tools to capture the attention of your customers. But, the most important sales pitch has not even taken place yet!

In retailing, it is only when your customer sets foot in the shop that all your marketing efforts could lead to a sale.

It is here that merchandise presentation, visual merchandising and customer service work in tandem with your marketing efforts (that is, advertising, promotions and so on) in a last-chance opportunity to influence your customer before a purchase decision is made.

—— Merchandise Presentation

Merchandise presentation refers to the most basic way of presenting merchandise in an orderly, understandable, easy-to-shop and easy-to-find format. It is the arrangement of merchandise by style, price point, saleability and inventory.

Merchandise presentation is also that part of the shop that remains constant longer than the visual presentation or display of a product. It

A merchandise presentation (courtesy of the Robinsons Group of Stores)

may not be the part of a presentation or display area that is the most exciting. Its main purpose is to support and enhance the display in a neat and organised manner.

Here are some points to consider:

Point to note	Actions
1. **Merchandise should be logically arranged**	• Similar merchandise should be grouped together in displays. • The best-selling spot should be reserved for merchandise that brings in the most profit and not for merchandise carrying the highest profit margins. • Merchandise that is heavy, bulky and fragile should be placed near the end of the shop.
2. **Merchandise should be categorised and displayed according to the customer's intention to buy**	• Merchandise purchased daily should be placed near the entrance to start the customer buying. • High-profit margin and impulse purchases should be placed alongside the basic demand merchandise. • Seasonal merchandise should be placed in prominent locations to encourage impulse buying.

Point to note	Actions
3. Merchandise should be displayed with impact	• Identical merchandise should be mass displayed. • Some merchandise should not be displayed too symmetrically. • Point-of-sale material should not be excessively used.
4. Merchandise should be presentable	• Merchandise should be regularly cleaned and dusted. • Merchandise should always be facing the customers.
5. Damaged merchandise should never be on a normal display	• Damaged merchandise may be sold at a discount in a bargain gondola or corner, and the customers must be informed about the state of the merchandise. Otherwise, such damaged merchandise should be removed.
6. Merchandise should be easily accessible	• Displays, particularly of basic merchandise, should not be changed too often. However, the display of seasonal merchandise can be changed frequently to create a 'new' look. • The amount of merchandise displayed should be in proportion to its sales and stockturn.
7. Merchandise should be displayed on correct equipment	• Correct and proper fixtures should be used for merchandise display. • There should be enough space between the fixtures to allow customers to browse.

Arrangement of merchandise by brand (courtesy of Aussino Group Ltd)

RETAIL OPERATIONS

Visual Presentation

A merchandise display (courtesy of Aussino Group Ltd)

Visual presentation is often referred to as display. It includes all merchandise not displayed in a permanent shelf location. It complements the basic merchandise presentation on a fixture or a wall area.

Displays are used to add interest and excitement to the shop.

They improve the shop's atmosphere and help to reinforce the shop's image.

The proper use of visual presentation to enhance merchandise within the shop can induce single or multiple sales. When a variety of merchandise is put together, they can offer customers a means of understanding as to how each item works, as well as how it enhances or supports the others.

For example, if you are selling cookware, you can enhance the display by adding cookbooks, aprons, utensils and even food. You could add a mannequin, for the human touch, wearing a T-shirt and an apron. You could also add a piece of furniture, tablecloth and napkins.

Cross merchandising
(courtesy of the Robinsons
Group of Stores)

Extending a display to incorporate related merchandise (cross-merchandising) is a very powerful selling tool.

Many elements go into the building of an effective display.

Merely grouping merchandise together will not make an attractive display.

When arranging the merchandise, the message to be sent out must be clear. The presentation must be focused. A customer will not remember a display if it shows a representation of all the available products, packed with other merchandise. The less busy and the more cohesive the display, the more likely your customers will notice what you are trying to sell.

A good display should incorporate the following:

- Have a theme (to stimulate a desire to buy and to integrate all marketing efforts, from the website to the shopping bags, sending coordinated and cohesive messages about the business, merchandise and services)

- Should provide information (for example, the description, location and price of merchandise on display)

A bed-linen display – An unorthodox way of attracting customers' attention
(courtesy of the Robinsons Group of Stores)

Mothers' Day gifts display
(courtesy of the Robinsons Group of Stores)

- Should be distinctive (do something different to promote impulse or unplanned purchases)

- Show the merchandise in use (to mould customer perceptions and influence buying behaviour)

A window display

- Must be maintained (keep display clean and neat to help promote the shop's image)

- Must be changed frequently (to launch new merchandise or promote existing merchandise)

Consider the following when creating a successful display:

- Identify the area and space for display within the shop (windows, tops and endcaps of the fixtures, walls, cashier counter)

- Determine the message to be sent out to the customer (a sale, promotion, launch of new merchandise)

- Identify the merchandise to be displayed (main focus) and select some merchandise to complement the display (secondary focus)

- Choose the appropriate props to support or add interest to the merchandise (for example, use appropriate cubes or boxes to bring display merchandise to the eye level)

- Determine the information to include in the sign, keeping in mind that it should be simple (for example, the brand or product, the special price, the normal price and the selling message)

- Identify the day and time needed to set up the display

- Review the display and also ensure that the lighting highlights the main focus of the display

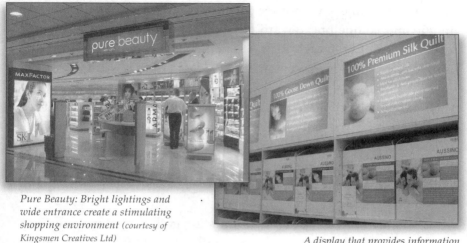

Pure Beauty: Bright lightings and wide entrance create a stimulating shopping environment (courtesy of Kingsmen Creatives Ltd)

A display that provides information (courtesy of Aussino Group Ltd)

- Update the display (for example, ensure that the displayed merchandise is replaced, should the merchandise become out of stock)

Customer Loyalty Scheme

A loyalty scheme is a mechanism to identify and reward loyal customers. It uses some form of membership card which is presented at the point of sale so as to obtain direct cash discount or record the value of a purchase to earn reward points for redemption of products or services.

Many retailers use loyalty scheme to retain or expand their customer base. The loyalty card is so common nowadays that it has become a commodity. It has remained questionable as to whether loyalty schemes have radically changed customer behaviour over time and contributed to the company's profitability.

Very often, retailers who offer loyalty programmes fail to create a unique and compelling reward for their target customers. They may set the threshold too high for customers to achieve rewards or create unnecessary barriers for customers to redeem their rewards.

Many retailers also fail to manage the loyalty scheme properly. They assume price is the only key motivator for a customer to make a purchase and thus, the loyalty scheme becomes merely a discount programme. There are no follow-up activities or events for customers in the loyalty scheme.

Others do not use the customer information gathered effectively. They assume a 'one-size-fits-all' scheme will work. Different customers want different things from the loyalty scheme.

A loyalty scheme should be individually tailored to meet your specific objectives and satisfy your valuable customers.

The most important success factor
for a loyalty programme is that
the reward must connect
the customer to the brand and
motivate the consumer to earn
the reward in the first place.

To establish a successful loyalty scheme, the retailer must first define the objective of the loyalty scheme. Different objectives will lead to different marketing efforts and thus different types of rewards to offer to various customer segments. Examples of loyalty scheme objectives include "to maximise spending per customer" or "to maximise retention of top spenders".

Secondly, the retailer must understand customers' motivation to buy, and encourage or 'reward' that behaviour to build loyalty. Examples of customer motivation to buy include convenience, special deals, special privileges, etc.

Thirdly, the retailer must analyse the customer information to establish some customer facts such as customers' buying patterns, lifestyles, and what could motivate and change their behaviour patterns in the store. In this case, the retailer can structure the rewards accordingly.

But, not all loyal customers would join the loyalty scheme. Some customers do not see the rewards as worthwhile. Others have no confidence in releasing their personal information to the company who is managing the scheme for fear of misuse. Hence, it should be noted that customer service is still one of the key ways to generate customer loyalty.

A loyalty scheme
cannot be a substitute for
customer service.

I need help...

How do I Improve my Shop's Personality?

What is it that draws a customer to one shop rather than another? Surely, there must be a force that is in operation besides the more obvious functional factors such as location, price and merchandise offerings.

This force is the shop's image. Shop image has a direct effect on the perceived value of your merchandise. It is the way in which the shop is defined in the shopper's mind, partly by its functional qualities and partly by psychological attributes. These include merchandise, location, promotion, pricing, service, clientele, atmosphere, layout and so on. When a customer enters your shop, he 'reads' your shop like a book. Often, those quiet spots are the floors, walls and ceiling. Your customer could be seeing everything you do not want them to notice.

1. Tangible factors

   - Availability of new merchandise
   - Breadth and depth of merchandise
   - Easy refund or exchange
   - Fast checkouts
   - Minimum out-of-stocks
   - Product quality
   - Sufficient sales assistance

2. Intangible factors

- Cleanliness

- Friendliness

- Helpfulness

- Neatness

- Trustworthiness

Ways to Improve Your Shop's Image at No Cost

- Always smile at your customers.

- Be nice to new customers.

- Allow customers to use your toilets if possible.

- Carry out regular housekeeping both internally and externally.

- Ensure that your shops exterior, especially the signage and lightings, is bright and inviting.

- Keep your window display attractive and simple. Make subtle changes to your windows weekly. Go 'window shopping' and borrow ideas from other retailers if necessary.

Time to Change Your Shop's Look?

- If you have not repainted or renovated your shop for many years, it is probably the time to do so. When in doubt, use a light colour to make your shop look cheery.

- Repair or replace faulty lightings and display fixtures, cracked tiles or worn carpet.

Responsible Retailing

14

In today's retailing environment, a retailer must concentrate not just on selling but also on being aware of some vital duties fundamental to successful retailing. This chapter highlights three important issues.

Ethical Issues

In any customer-oriented business.

Professionalism,
efficiency,
speed and
reliability are
vital elements.

Thus it will be useful if the retailer is aware of some general retail practices which may or may not have legal implications. These practices will serve to enhance Singapore's reputation as a shoppers' paradise.

Here are some points to ponder on:

An ethical retailer should:

1. Display and disclose all relevant information on the price tags

2. Mark merchandise prices in Singapore currency

3. Sell merchandise at reasonable prices

4. Issue receipts for all merchandise sold

5. Provide good sales and after-sales service

6. Respond promptly to all customer complaints

7. Ensure that all employees are informed of the merchandise and store policies.

An ethical retailer should not:

1. Sell any counterfeit merchandise

2. Misrepresent any information relating to the merchandise

3. Engage touts to promote the business

4. Impose a surcharge on the use of charge or credit cards

— Legal Issues

The proliferation of consumer protection, under civil and criminal law, implies that it is in the interest of all retailers to be knowledgeable about the law as it affects them in their daily dealings with customers. This section aims to give retailers some awareness of the current legal environment affecting retail operations.

Area Of Concern	Source	Description
Advertising	1. The Singapore Code of Advertising Practice	1. A set of rules that covers not only matters such as offensive advertisements but also particular issues that arise from advertising certain products such as medicine and alcohol.
Merchandising	1. Medicine Act and Smoking (Control of Advertisement and Sale of Tobacco) Act	1. Laws that require merchandise to be labelled correctly.
	2. Licensing agreements	2. Agreements that allow retailers to sell products or services made by others in return for royalty payments.
	3. Merchandise restrictions	3. Constraints on selling certain specified goods or services.
	4. Product guarantees and warranties	4. Obligations to honour the terms and conditions stated.
	5. Sale of Goods Act	5. Liable to be sued if retailers sell defective products.
		Retailers who sell products that have not been adequately tested or that have been declared unsafe are liable to be penalised..
	6. Copyright Act and Trademarks Act	6. Laws that concern the exclusive rights to brand names developed.
		Laws that concern intellectual property rights.

Area Of Concern	Source	Description
Pricing	1. Goods and Services Act	1. Laws relating to the taxation of goods and services in Singapore.
Retail selling	1. Copyright Act	1. Provisions on parallel imports in Singapore as implied in the Copyright Act.
	2. Multi-Level Marketing and Pyramid Selling (Prohibition) Act	2. Laws that prohibit the registration of businesses that are designed to promote multi-level marketing schemes.
	3. Sale of Goods Act	3. Laws that govern the sale of merchandise.
	4. Small Claims Tribunal Act	4. The tribunal is accessible to any consumer or trader who has a claim not exceeding S$10,000 arising from any contract for the sale of goods or the provision of services.
Store location	1. Zoning laws	1. Laws that restrict the use of a location for certain types of businesses and the types of facilities that may be constructed.
	2. Leases and mortgages	2. Laws requiring the compliance of the stipulations in leases, tenancy agreements and mortgage documentation.
Store operations	1. Income Tax Act	1. Laws relating to income tax, real estate tax and property tax.
	2. Franchise agreements	2. Laws relating to the rights and obligations of the franchisor and franchisee.
	3. Employment Act	3. Laws relating to the hiring of personnel with certain minimum qualifications in certain retail businesses.
		Laws relating to the dismissal of employees.

The Consumer Protection (Fair Trading) Act

With the introduction of the Consumer Protection (Fair Trading) Act, consumers will be able to sue for monetary compensation by simply showing that the traders have committed dishonest practices. The Second Schedule of the Act specifies 20 unfair practices.

Generally, these unfair practices cover three main areas of trade:

1. False or misleading advertising such as:

    • Hiding or lying about important product information

    • Trying to attract shoppers by promoting an offer that the traders know they cannot deliver

    • Using small print to conceal a material fact from the customer

2. False bargains such as:

    • Lying about the duration of a promotion or a sale

    • Putting up 'closing down sale' signs when the trader has no intention to end the business

    • Raising the prices of merchandise just before a sale

3. Unethical sales practices such as:

- Harassing or pressuring people to buy a product
- Withdrawing free gifts that have been promised prior to the purchase
- Including in a consumer agreement, terms or conditions that are harsh or excessively one-sided

It is clear from the above mentioned that the trader should provide the consumer with all relevant information so as not to mislead the consumer. The consumer can then make an informed decision. As such, the trader should begin reviewing his business practices, particularly the type of information to provide or convey to the consumers.

However, consumers will not be the only ones to benefit. By marking out the minimum standards of business practices, the traders will also benefit. The Act protects traders from unreasonable consumers and unscrupulous competitors.

It is important to note that the Act covers all consumer goods and services with the exception of some transactions:

- Financial investments
- Purchase and sale of property
- Transactions with value that exceeds S$20,000

A full copy of the Consumer Protection (Fair Trading) Act may be downloaded from the Internet at www.mti.gov.sg.

I need help...

How can I Avoid the Legal Pitfalls of Irresponsible Advertising?

An advertisement is a powerful tool and can do wonders for the image and sales figures of a business provided, of course, it is well designed and appropriately displayed.

All too often, an irresponsibly designed advertisement gives rise to legal liability, usually for defamation, especially when the retailer, in the course of promoting his own product or service, unwittingly insults a competitor. As such, it is

important for a retailer
to be always mindful of
the potential liability

each time it decides
to advertise its
product or service.

Common Irresponsible Advertising Practices of Retailers

1. **Puffery**

   'Puffery' is where the advertiser describes his goods with dubious qualities using phrases such as 'the best in the world' and 'super quality'. Under the Consumer Protection (Fair Trading) Act, 'representing that goods or services are of a particular standard, quality, grade.... if they are not' is a specific act that would be considered wrongful under the Act. Therefore, it is arguable that puffery may be caught by this prohibition.

2. **Subliminal advertising**

   This is an advertising method that works on the subconscious of the shopper, ranging from hidden verbal communications in piped music to ultra-fast flashing images at the cinema. As far as this particular form of advertising is concerned, the Act is less clear. While there seems to be no specific reference to this form of advertising, it is possible that it may be caught under the provision in the Act which makes it unlawful for retailers to take advantage of a consumer by 'exerting undue pressure or undue influence on the consumer to enter into a transaction involving goods or services'. This, of course, depends on whether subliminal advertising can indeed have the effect of exerting undue pressure or undue influence on a shopper.

Practical Steps to Take to Avoid Legal Liability

1. **Engage a professional to design the advertisement**

   Choosing a reputable advertising agency will minimise the risk of liability. If the design is undertaken by the retailer or the staff, care should be taken to ensure that it does not offend competitors in any way.

2. **Have a lawyer vet the proposed advertisement**

Although this may seem to be an overly cautious step, it may well be one worth taking if there is any doubt at all as to whether the advertisement (whether by virtue of its content or presentation) may amount to an infringement of copyright.

Lastly, ensure that advertisements are not offensive. It is important to ensure that your advertisements do not inadvertently or otherwise amount to a debasement of public morals and taste, especially in the advertising and promotion of products such as alcohol, the very nature of which tends to lend itself to irresponsible advertising. While these advertisements are not illegal, a responsible advertiser should take ethical considerations into account. An advertisement done in poor taste will not attract legal liability but may well cost the company hard-earned customer goodwill.

By Patricia Moreira, Lecturer, School of Business

Information Technology and Retailing

The business environment has undergone many changes, triggered by new technologies, new products and the ever-increasing demands of more sophisticated consumers. How can retailers cope with the changes? How can they prepare and position themselves to face the turbulent marketplace?

Information technology (IT) is the answer.

> Sufficient and up-to-date information derived from the use of IT systems helps retailers analyse the changes and embark on the best decisions for their company.

Where can retailers start? How do they look for a suitable system for the business? How can they really benefit and see results? This chapter aims to answer these questions.

Retail IT can be categorised into two types:

1. **Point-of-Sale (POS) systems**

2. **Other electronic applications**, such as the Internet and electronic commerce, and interactive kiosks.

— Point-Of-Sale Systems

There are three main areas that retailers need to be aware of before they source and adopt any information system in their company.

- Type of System

- Front-end versus Back-end Systems

- Benefits of IT

Type of System

POS is the working terminal at the front of the store. It captures important information relating to sales, products and customers. Some systems contain only the POS element — built only to record sales and do look-ups. There are two types of systems:

1. **Standalone system**

    There are 'standalone' merchandising, POS, customer profiling and financial systems in the market. Some large retailers purchase these four systems separately and then integrate the systems on their own.

2. **Integrated System**

    There are also integrated retail systems that have all the four components already combined. It is better for small retailers with no IT expertise to buy an integrated package where they do not need to write interfaces between POS, merchandising, customer profiling and financials. Moreover, retailers can find many retail systems that can be tailored specifically for their type of business.

Whichever system the retailers are considering, they should choose a system that is:

- proven with positive track record for years in many other stores
- easy to use and train personnel
- suitable for unique operation and business format
- supported by top professional technicians located near them
- thoroughly documented
- ready to accommodate their future expansion
- built on standard current technology
- affordable and competitively priced

Front-End versus Back-End Systems

Where should IT begin? Retailers have to understand the back-end versus front-end issues in IT applications.

1. **Back-end system**

    Retailers need to link the POS system to the back-end office system. However, it is not necessary to have a head office or back-end office. There are many small and single retailers who install the IT system at the shopfront. In such a case, the back-end application is incorporated into the front-end system.

    Merchandise should ideally have either a Universal Product Code (UPC) or a store-generated barcode. A retailer can create his own barcodes for his products by assigning numerical symbols to vendor, and product descriptions such as department, item and style. The barcode is then created with a bar code machine. Alternatively, retailers without a bar code machine can just use numerical symbols.

Before the retailer can start using the POS system to generate any data for meaningful analysis, he needs a back-end office system to scan and key in the following data:

- Inventory data: Purchase orders, delivery orders, product code's, descriptions, cost and selling prices, returns to suppliers

- Operations perimeter: Cashier's identity and password, discount limit for cashier and/or manager, minimum and maximum float amount, maximum quantities for repeat orders

- Customer information: Retailers can pre-determine and key in the perimeters used for customer database; for example, amount purchased per transaction, residential estates (for trading area analysis), gender

- Vendor information: Name and address of vendor, contact numbers, trade discount.

2.   **Front-end system**

POS systems are not merely cash registers that retailers can use to key in sales. With the support of back-end systems, the front-end POS terminal captures sales, inventory and customer data instantly, and tracks the movement of products within a retail organisation. This provides retailers with up-to-the-minute information such as what is selling best and what is not selling. This leads to better and faster decisions on re-orders and markdowns.

Benefits of IT

There are numerous benefits that can be derived from the application of IT systems.

1.   **Customer satisfaction**

> The checkout area is a profit centre where a customer's last impression is created.

Customers do not like to wait long to make their payment.

A good POS system speeds up the checkout process and facilitates efficiency and accuracy in totalling customers' purchases.

Sometimes, customers inquire about quantity balance, colours and size for a product. Cashiers can utilise the POS system to look up information so as to respond to the customers without delay.

> Some systems offer the opportunity for add-on sale.

When an item, for example, a bottle of nail colour, is scanned, the system features a list of related items such as nail colour remover, nail art accessories and cuticle cream on the screen. This prompts the sales staff to suggest any item from the list to the customer.

2. Better management control
The Management will be able to analyse the information received from the systems, identify problems or opportunities, and make decisions or changes for the company without delay.

Some areas of benefits include the following:

Types of Information	Benefits
Itemised sale transaction	Retailers are no longer restricted to departmental analysis of sales each day, but know exactly which items were sold and which need re-ordering. It allows for trend analysis of saleable items, which ultimately benefits inventory management.
Sales reports	Detailed database of sales and stock not only helps retailers analyse product mix, but also assists buying and merchandising staff produce finely tuned forecasts and budgets. This will help retailers improve their merchandise stockturn and thus enhance profits. Some systems, for example, the Retail Pro software system, are able to generate graphic reports in the form of graphs and charts.
Buyers' purchase records	Computerised purchase orders keep track of the merchandiser's buying activities. Management can also have information on the purchase quantity and dollar value.
Stock list	Stock-on-hand reports showing updated balance assist both buyers and sales personnel in the area of inventory management, sales floor stock replenishment, shelf allocation and customer service.
Cashier activity	The data helps management monitor cashier activity and, prevent fraud. The system is able to check the number of sales, void, refund and exchange transactions performed by a particular cashier.

In a chain store, the information being transmitted from the front-end system of the various stores is received in a timely manner and accurately because the IT system checks for errors. In addition, the data received from the stores are automatically fed into the back-end system. Hence, clerical errors can be reduced as data from the stores do not need to be keyed in again.

The next few pages will showcase examples of reports derived from POS system, courtesy of *Integrated Retail Management Consulting Pte Ltd.*

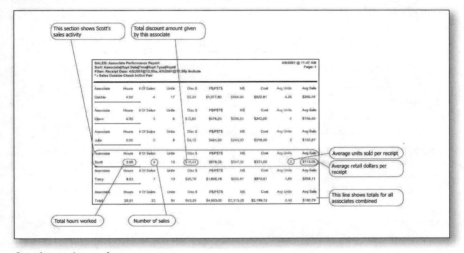

Sample associate performance report

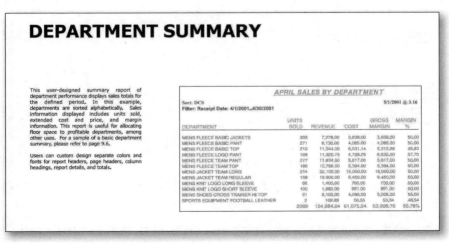

Sample department summary report

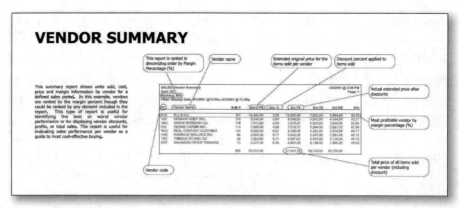

Sample vendor summary report

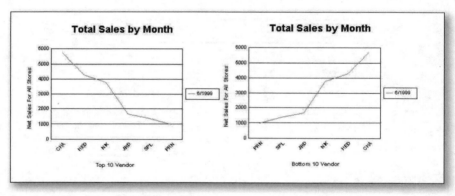

Sample vendor sales performance (graph)

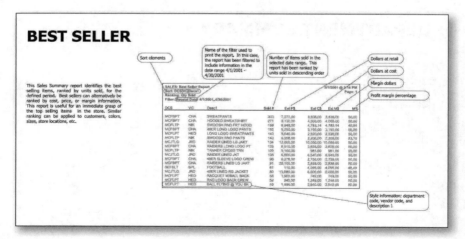

Sample best seller report

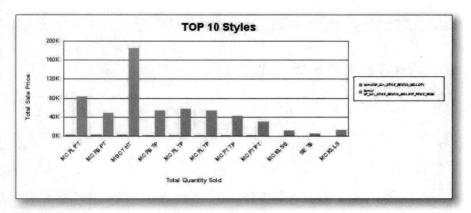

Sample top 10 style

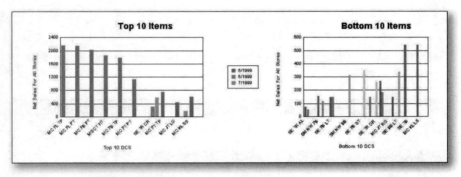

Sample top 10 bottom (graph)

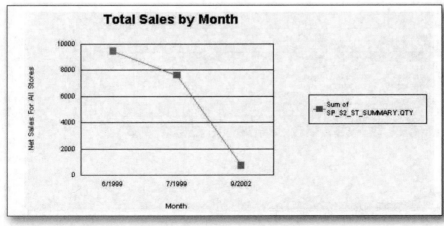

Sample monthly sales summary

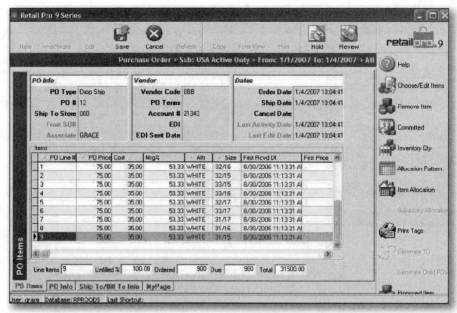

Sample purchase order

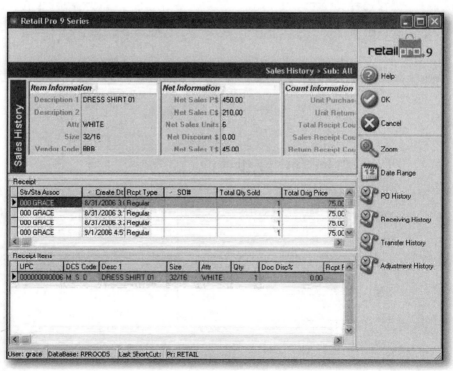

Sample inventory item sales history

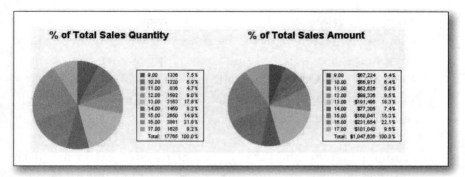

Sample hourly sales summary

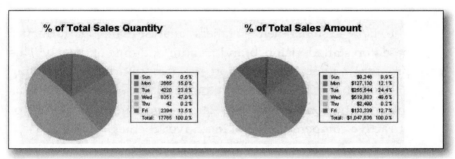

Sample sales day summary

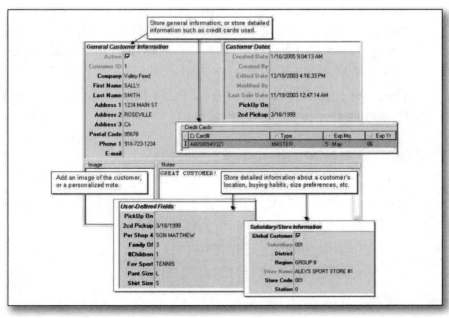

Sample customer record

3. **Manpower planning**

    Computer systems have become more powerful. Many companies are able to find new applications that benefit them directly. One such application is the labour scheduling programme that helps managers develop the labour schedule or roster for the stores.

    Scanning systems and POS systems help cashiers scan and place the merchandise into the carrier bags at the same time. This enhances manpower planning and reduces cost directly.

    The POS systems help retailers analyse sales performance based on staff, division, brand, vendor and time of the day. This provides valuable information for a more accurate planning on manpower needs during the different shifts, as well as the realistic forecast of sales targets, and implementation of attractive compensation and incentive schemes.

4. **Customer relationship**

    Retailers combine information about customer shopping patterns and preferences from their own sales information with commercially available databases on demographics, national shopping surveys and trading areas so as to improve customer targeting and promotions.

    The more innovative retailers even use the IT systems to integrate their customer loyalty programme.

    The data collected helps to identify regular customers and provide knowledge on what they buy and how much they spend on each shopping trip.

Data such as the most saleable or least saleable merchandise help retailers to plan for promotions to increase sales. Retailers can either implement programmes to sell unpopular items or introduce promotional activities related to the popular items to increase customer patronage and sales.

5. **Supplier relationship**
   IT systems have facilitated direct sending of invoices and purchase orders between suppliers and retailers. In addition, the supplier can notify the retailer about stock balance, suitable order quantity, recommended retail pricing, new product launch, and sales promotions and advertising.

6. **Better communication with employees**
   Back-end systems improve communication with store employees, district or area managers, and staff at headquarters through the use of electronic mail. Up-to-date information on price change, new promotion mechanisms and purchase orders can be transmitted to the employees.

7. **Improved company image**
   The benefits derived from the use of an appropriate IT system together with good business practices will ultimately enhance the shop's image. Generally, customers feel that retailers that use IT systems are more productive and reliable.

▬ Internet Technology

Retailers can utilise many other technological applications to sell their products and services directly to consumers. Small retailers should view direct sales as an opportunity, and not as a threat or a burden to their current operations strategies.

In addition,

> the younger generation of customers are becoming more IT-savvy. They surf the Internet not only to source for information, but also to shop for new products.

Thus small retailers cannot ignore the growth potential in the Internet business that is referred to as e-retailing.

Internal Communication Tools

Retailers can use the Internet to share information among employees and to train the staff internally. This technology has been labelled as 'Intranet'. Employees will be informed in a timely manner of the latest development or changes in the organisation. The information includes changes in price, product delivery and customer programmes. Thus the sales staff will be able to carry out their duties and responsibilities more efficiently.

Setting Up Shop Online

Generally, setting up an online shop requires immense technical expertise and capital. Larger retailers can purchase their own server and e-commerce software to run the whole entity themselves. However, there is an easier and cheaper way available to small retailers who just want to try out their business on the Web.

There are a number of online portals on the Web available to the retailer to build an online store and run it. Examples of such portals are Yahoo! and MSN Singapore. In addition, there is also a variety of e-commerce solutions suppliers that provide packages to help retailers set up shop online. Retailers can find out more on how to set up an online shop from the Internet.

It may be worthwhile to employ professionals to help set up the online store initially. However, it is useful to the implementation of e-retailing if the retailer is aware of some basic considerations before and after setting up an online store.

1. Before setting up an online store
   - *Develop a business plan for the e-business:* Internet retailing involves as much commitment as store retailing.

   - *Obtain a domain name for the website:* The website address has to be related to the store so that customers can recall it without much difficulty.

   - *Create an interesting home page:* Visit other online stores for ideas. Use good pictures.

   - *Make the site credit-card friendly:* It is a common practice to accept credit cards for payment, and customers must feel the convenience and security when they use their credit card online. A merchant account is needed to process credit card transactions and deposit revenue in the bank. It is important to contact the bank for more details on this issue.

   - *Offer delivery or shipping service:* An attractive site with interesting products may induce customers to buy, but a fast and hassle-free delivery service generates repeat business.

   - *Promote the online store:* Register with one or a few portals and/or search engines to attract customers to the online store.

2. **After setting up an online store**

Once the online store is in operation, the next important thing is to maintain and sustain the site. How do you attract customers to visit your site frequently and to make purchases? Here are some tips to ensure the success of the e-business:

- *Create a user-friendly site:* Ensure that the shop's contact details are available and keep the opening pages clean and simple.

- *Minimise the customer's access time:* Online stores with fanciful designs such as whirling graphics, gyrating buttons, flashing banners and 3D pictures can actually slow down loading time.

- *Respond to buyers as soon as possible:* Check your e-mails frequently to answer all customers' queries promptly.

- *Check out your competitors' sites:* Visit your competitors' sites to see how you can offer better value to your customers.

- *Market your online store:* Advertise your store online with the help of online portal and search engines. Display the address of your website prominently on your shopping bags, letterhead, receipts, cash memo and print advertisements.

- *Analyse reports:* Track and monitor the number of visits to and sales from the website, and analyse the reports to improve business.

- *Update and maintain your site regularly:* Customers get tired of seeing the same thing, so always keep your site updated.

Selling and Promotion

Retailers do not have to offer customers the option to buy online. There are small retailers who have no intention to sell online. Instead they utilise the Internet as a platform for advertisement and promotion.

Promote the store's presence and educate customers about the store's products and services by providing information on:

- store's address and contact numbers
- products sizes, colours, availability and prices
- services such as exchange policy, reservation procedures, repair and alteration, delivery, gift-wrapping and complaint resolution
- promotional activities such as discounts, festive specials, purchase-with-purchase, free redemptions and new product launches

Provide value-added information related to the store and products:
- Advice on latest product trends
- Tips on smart buying and saving
- Information on new store images
- Ideas on buying creative gifts

— Interactive Kiosks

Interactive kiosks are free-standing computerised terminals located inside the stores. These kiosks provide consumers with information on merchandise, services, prices, promotional programmes and the latest product offerings. The consumers can then check for stock availability, place their orders directly and make requests for delivery to their homes.

Retailers can use the kiosks to provide specific product information.

For example, an apparel retailer can use the kiosks to provide wardrobe tips on the colour, style of clothing and the fabric suitable for various body shapes. They can even provide information on the latest fashion trend.

For innovative retailers, they can add value by providing additional entertainment news

such as new music releases, concert information, new release of video clips and sports updates through the kiosks.

The ability to mix their own products and services with entertainment will definitely enhance the retailer's image and increase sales.

Additional Technology Applications

There are other technology applications that retailers can adopt to enhance their operations. Here are some examples:

- Scanning devices

- Handheld electronic inventory and re-ordering equipment

- Computer-controlled electronic billboards and mannequins

- Cyberspace retailing

- Interactive television

- Virtual showrooms

- Mobile handheld payment system

Misconceptions about IT Systems

Owing to some misconceptions, many small retailers do not see the need to introduce IT in their businesses.

Misconception 1
IT applications are often viewed as complicated. Retailers worry that they cannot comprehend the sophisticated IT systems and operations.

TRUTH!
There are POS systems that are user-friendly and provide online step-by-step guidance to retailers. The Retail Pro software system is one such example.

Retailers tend to equate sophistication to complication. A system may be sophisticated because of its ability to perform many tasks. Retailers sometimes feel overwhelmed by the sudden influx of information.

Misconception 2

IT systems are expensive. Retailers feel that will incur a huge capital investment using IT applications and are afraid that the returns may not be forthcoming after the introduction of IT systems into their businesses.

TRUTH!

Adoption of IT systems may incur high initial cost, but the cost may be insignificant compared with the amount of savings that can be derived from accurate data analysis.

Dollar store and value store retailers that sell thousands of items at one price or a low price are ideal candidates for computerisation because they have a lot of inventory and face low margins. Due to intense competition, these types of retailers need to keep up-to-date with merchandise information to stock their shelves with saleable merchandise.

Misconception 3

IT systems are only suitable for large retail stores. They need the system to help them maintain procedures and stock. In addition, the bigger retailers have the manpower and expertise to handle the IT function in the company.

TRUTH!

Small retail businesses also have to maintain their operational procedures and stock. Customers who walk into a store expect good service and stock availability regardless of the size of the store. In fact, an efficient system lays the foundation for future expansion — a consistent inventory and sales management system for all outlets is very important in monitoring the performance of the outlets.

It is true that large retailers have IT specialists to handle the implementation and problems of IT systems. However, small retailers can overcome this problem by training their staff. IT system companies realise that retailers who benefit from their software programmes are actually excellent advertisement for them. Hence, the IT companies are willing to provide comprehensive training for the retailers' staff to ensure a successful implementation of the IT system.

Misconception 4

IT applications are massive and provide generic information on sales, inventory and marketing. There are no custom-made applications that serve a specific retailer's needs.

TRUTH!

There are IT systems that offer custom-made applications to meet the specific needs of small retailers. For example, Retail Pro software packages have been specifically developed for speciality retailers of apparel, footwear, accessories, gifts, sporting goods, house ware, toys, jewellery, home furnishings and the general retail store (refer to 'I need help' at the end of the chapter for more information).

— Challenges Ahead

Before retailers can decide on what they would like to do next, they have to understand the following issues.

1. **Back to basics (the importance of procedures)**
    No retailer should start installing an IT system without having the fundamental operational and merchandising procedures in place. In fact, many retailers use the IT system to help them formulate effective and efficient business procedures for their stores.

2. **Determine needs and direction**
    Retailers must be able to answer the following questions to guide them in their search for the most suitable system.

    *   What is the plan for an IT system in the company?

    *   What are the benefits that are important to the company at this moment?

- What types of information are needed by the company to improve operations and sales?

Prior to the installation of the system, the retailer has to provide such necessary information to aid the system engineer to configure the system to meet the retailer's needs.

3. **Implications for the future**

It is a fact that the use of IT applications will improve employee productivity, customer satisfaction and sales performance. With the availability and constant falling prices of new technology, small retailers can afford to utilise high-powered personal computers, retail-based computer software and other basic technology that provide up-to-date information to start a website as well as to improve their competitiveness. Small retailers may even use the technological advances as a distinctive feature to attract and add value to customers, and ultimately, to differentiate themselves from the other retailers.

I need help...

Can you show me an
Excellent Software System for Retailers?

Retail Pro is an example of a sophisticated software package used by many retailers.

Retail Pro manages
front- to back-end
retail operations seamlessly,

from the point of sale and customer management to purchasing, receiving, tagging, inventory control, distribution, supplier management and reports analysis.

The software caters to both independent single store's and multinational retail chains with hundreds of outlets. In order to be able to accomplish their task, Retail Pro has developed distinct software editions that provide the level of functionality required by different business formats.

1. **Retail Pro Shop Edition:** A system for retail entrepreneurs managing one to three shops

2. **Retail Pro Merchant Edition:** A system that is ideal for established retail operations, from a single location up to 20 stores and/or franchisees

3. **Retail Pro Corporate Edition:** A powerful Oracle-based solution for large stores and multinational chains operating across regions

Each Retail Pro edition scales smoothly up to the next, thus allowing a retailer who wants to expand the flexibility to incorporate the next edition into the current edition.

Some of the additional benefits derived from the Retail Pro system are:

- **'Hot seller' report:** With this report, retailers can look up items in the inventory with a sell-through of greater than 50 percent, or ask for the top 5, 20 or 100 best-selling items.

- **'Coldest items' report:** With this report, retailers can either mark down the slow-moving items or return them to the suppliers.

- **Additional information on the receipt:** In addition to product description and cost, the receipt can also feature additional information about the VIP customer such as special discounts, credit points for gift redemptions and so on. The information facilitates and complements promotional activities.

- **'Related item' feature:** When an item, for example, a bottle of nail colour, is scanned, the system features a list of related items such as nail colour remover, nail art accessories and cuticle cream on the screen. This prompts the sales staff to suggest any item from the list to the customer. This provides an excellent opportunity for add-on sale.

- **Average transaction report:** The system can calculate the average transaction daily. This information is a critical measurement of a store's productivity.

- **'Missing person' report:** The system can help retailers find their missing customers —customers who used to be regular but have not visited the store for some time. For example, the system allows a retailer to enter the database and find every customer who spent more than $200 in the store last year, who has visited the store more than five times, but who has not visited the store in the past four months. The retailer can then follow up with a letter to invite the 'missing customer' to the store, and even enclose a gift certificate to encourage him to return.

In Singapore, retailers using Retail Pro include *77th Street, Cerisi, Country Road, GG<5, Hugo Boss, Pretty Fit, Mothercare, Sim Siang Choon Hardware, Swarovski* and many others.

RETAIL OPERATIONS

Organisation and People Management

A retail organisation, whether big or small, must be well-organised and the employees must be effectively managed.

Since many small retailers are mainly family-operated businesses and hire only a few workers, they tend to think that there is no need to have any organisational structure. They prefer to conduct their businesses on an informal basis, which gives rise to ill-defined roles and inappropriate practices.

At the same time, retailers often lament that staff turnover is too high and so they do not spend effort in managing their employees. There are no company policies and procedures pertaining to personnel management. This results in unmotivated workers who feel that the company does not care about their welfare, and so leave for better opportunities elsewhere.

The following discussions aim to raise awareness of issues relating to the development of organisational structure, building of company or shop culture, and management of employees, all of which are applicable to both big and small retailers.

━━ Organisational Structure

In order to achieve co-ordination and control, a retailer has to plan for the following:

1. **Identify jobs based on the following categories:**
   - Function (operations, buying, delivery)
   - Product (gifts, ladieswear, housewares)
   - Geographic (locations of outlets)
   - Combination of the above

   It is common for a small retailer to hire an employee who is able to multi-task; for example, the store supervisor may be incharge of operations, buying, training and coordinating delivery at the same time.

2. **Develop inter-relationships among the various positions**
    Individual employees have their own jobs to perform, but at the same time, they need to coordinate with one another and work together to build a successful business.

3. **Outline the hierarchy of authority**
    The reporting relationship among the employees, from the lowest to the highest level, has to be clearly defined. A small retailer usually has only two to three levels of personnel.

4. **Create an organisation chart**
    An organisation chart graphically displays a retail organisation's hierarchical relationships. It is useful to display the chart in the shop (perhaps at the back office) so that the employees are aware of the hierarchy of authority. The following charts show the organisations of two small retailers.

ORGANISATION CHART FOR A MINI-MART

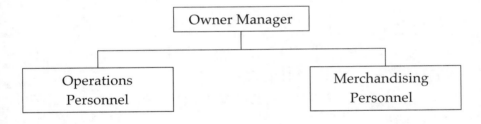

ORGANISATION CHART FOR A FURNITURE CHAIN

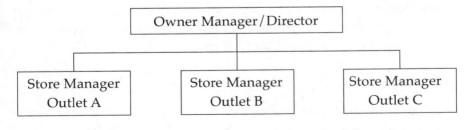

— Culture Development

A retail organisation comprises employees from varied backgrounds and of different personalities. These employees have their own set of beliefs and values. How can a retail organisation develop a common identity among the employees? What should be done to create a unique image perceived by the customers? The answer lies in the development of an organisational culture.

A retail organisation, whether big or small, has to develop its own culture.

> Organisational culture is similar to a person's personality. It reflects a company's vision and mission,

which are often created by the owner and senior management.

> It is a common system of values and practice evolved in the company. It provides guidance on what can and cannot be done.

Small retailers often have the misconception that culture is sophisticated and therefore meant only for big companies. Culture can be any value and practice that a small retailer identifies as beneficial to the growth and unity of the company.

Here is an example:

A neighbourhood grocery shop may be small, but the employees have to order, receive and replenish stocks, handle the POS system, serve customers, administer delivery, supervise staff and manage the finances. The employees merely carry out their respective duties. The owner may want to introduce the following principles and values to motivate the employees to work towards a common goal:

- **Honesty:** Employees should deal honestly with the customers.

- **Open communication:** Owner and manager should communicate store policies, procedures and problems to the staff.

- **Unity:** Employees should not blame one another when problems arise, but should work together to resolve the issue.

- **Responsibility:** Every employee should complete his task within the given time, and be responsible when handling a customer's requests.

- **Punctuality:** Employees should be punctual for work and respond to customers without delay.

The above values are the guiding principles for appropriate behaviours at the workplace. Both senior and junior staff should carry out the principles consistently. A particular image will evolve over time and become the culture of the shop.

The success will depend on the owner's conviction and persistence in the implementation.

— People Management

Employees carry out the operational and merchandising procedures, serve the customers and, to a certain extent, determine the image of the shop. As a small retailer, one of the most important tasks is to develop and train an effective and efficient workforce to conduct the business with good and consistent standards.

Every employee should receive the guidance, direction and support needed to perform the job productively. Suitable employees have to be recruited, trained, motivated and supervised.

At the same time, they have to be

fairly treated and compensated.

Recruiting the Potential Employee

Depending on the position, a retailer can find potential employees from the following sources:

- Educational institutions

- Competitors

- Other industries: People from another industry who possess suitable attributes and skills can be hired as they can provide fresh ideas and add value to the business.

- Employment agencies

- Recruitment advertisements

- Notices in the store: A small retailer may place notice of job vacancies outside the shop. However, such advertisements must be properly written and posted. A substandard, handwritten advertisement creates a bad impression for both the potential employee and the customers.

- Current workers: Sometimes, it is more productive to promote a current employee who is familiar with the shop procedures and culture.

- Employee referrals

Selecting the Right People

A Human Resource staff interviewing a potential employee

The retailer has to select
the person who matches
the job requirements and
the company culture.

While the retailer is choosing suitable candidates, these candidates are also evaluating the retailer as a potential employer through the selection process. Hence, it is important that the selection process be carried out in a professional manner. Retailers can use one or a combination of the following selection methods:

1. **Interview:** Retailers should be prepared for the interview — questions, venue and length of interview, attributes to look out for.

2. **Tests:** Larger retailers may utilise aptitude and integrity tests for management and security positions. A simple mathematical test may be useful for selecting cashiers.

3. **Reference checks:** Some retailers contact the references either prior to or after the interview to find out more about the potential candidate.

Retailing is a service-oriented industry.

People who desire to work in the retail industry have to possess certain qualities and attributes. Sales assistants and assistant cashiers may require personality traits such as:

- Cheerfulness

- Patience

- Honesty

- Pleasant grooming

Supervisors, store managers and merchandisers will require additional attributes such as:

- Analytical skills

- Creativity

- Flexibility

- Initiative

- Leadership

- Stress tolerance

Training and Developing the Employees

Small retailers are often apprehensive about training their staff. With rapid staff turnover, many retailers feel that it is a waste of resources to train the employees. There must be a paradigm shift.

Enhancing employees'
abilities to communicate with
customers, solve problems, sell the
products and carry out appropriate
operational procedures will help
increase customer
patronage and sales.

There are generally three types of training programmes.

1. Orientation programmes: When a new employee joins a retailer, he should be briefed on the company's history, policies, working hours, medical and fringe benefits, chain of command and job responsibilities. He should be introduced to the immediate superior and colleagues. Some retailers may even assign a mentor to guide the new employee.

Training and developing employees will help to increase sales

2. **General programmes:** Usually, general programmes comprise training related to the development of service quality, selling techniques, leadership skills and personal attributes.

3. **Specific programmes:** These are job-specific training such as POS system operations, cash and credit card handling, receiving and marking procedures, buying techniques and other operations procedures.

Retailers must also determine the following issues in the training programme:

- **Length of the training programme:** It varies from one- or two-day sessions to two-year programmes.

- **Training schedules for all the staff in a calendar year:** Some skills, for example, customer service, may require more frequent training. With the increase in customers' expectations, customer service skills must be constantly reinforced or updated.

- **Training needs of staff:** Retailers should identify the areas that need improvement or correction.

- **Format of training:** Retailers have to determine how the training should be conducted. Although training is often associated with classroom programmes, a small retailer may find the on-the-job training method more effective. The owner or manager can utilise the operational manuals to train the staff on the sales floor. In this way, staff do not need to be sent away but are still available on the sales floor to serve the customers. In addition, although programmes such as leadership skills and POS system operations may require external trainers, training related to the shop operations, communication and customer service may be conducted by the owner or the manager.

Compensating the Employees

Employees should perceive compensation as fair.

Rewards should be clearly related to the employees' work.

If excellent service is determined as important, then the employees should be rewarded based on how well they serve the customers. At the start, retailers should determine the assessment criteria and communicate this to the employees. The following tips provide retailers with some guidelines on the determination of compensation schemes:

- Retailers should develop a pay structure for different levels of position.

- Compensation can be based on individual and/or team performance.

- Generally, compensation is based on sales and profit earned. Retailers can also base incentives on more creative criteria, such as mystery shopper scores, good customer service (the number of compliments received by an individual employee), minimal discrepancies encountered by a cashier and lowest inventory shortages.

- There are various compensation methods.

  - Monetary payments such as salaries, commissions, bonuses and so on. A combination of monetary incentives may be used. For example, a ladieswear boutique may introduce a three-tier scheme — a basic salary, individual commission and a store bonus — for additional sales achieved.

  - Fringe benefits such as medical reimbursement, paid vacation, insurance benefits, additional annual leave, profit sharing and so on.

Supervising the Employees

A retailer who is too concerned about checking on staff movement — what time they report to work, what time they go for their break and how long they take for their break,

is simply
controlling the employees.
No supervision has taken place.

The objectives of supervision are to:

- improve productivity
- maintain employee morale
- motivate staff
- communicate store policies
- resolve problems
- reduce repetitive work
- monitor expenses

▬ Retailer's Options

From the above discussions, we can conclude that a healthy and growing retailer with motivated staff calls for the combination of a well-organised company, a strong shared culture among the employees, and an effective and efficient human resource management process.

Get regular feedback from your staff

For retailers who have never thought of these issues, it is time to pay attention to them. The following questions may be helpful for a start:

- Does the company have a vision and mission statement? If yes, are they communicated to all the staff?

- Are the lines of authority clear?

- Do employees know their respective responsibilities?

- Are the jobs and their respective scope of duties clearly described?

- Does the company have policies with regards to recruitment, selection, training, compensation and supervision of staff?

- How does the company hire staff?

- Are the employees feeling happy and satisfied? If yes, what are the factors that contributed to their satisfaction?

I need help...

Can you show me a Sample Recruitment Document?

A Sample Job Description for a Shop Supervisor

Job Position: Supervisor
Reports to: Shop Manager

Functions:

1. To assist the Shop Manager to manage the retail shop

2. To cover the Store Manager's duties in his absence

3. To maximise and achieve sales targets

Key Tasks:

1. **Sales**
    * Meet sales target
    * Monitor sales performance of products
    * Assist to serve customers

2. **Merchandising**
    * Monitor stock movements
        - Repeat order for fast-moving merchandise
        - Return slow-moving merchandise
    * Prepare floor plan as and when required

- Follow up on orders and ensure that new merchandise is displayed immediately and prominently
- Proposal of markdowns for slow-moving merchandise
- Regroup merchandise when the stock level is low
- Supervise receiving, checking, tagging and storage of merchandise

3. **Operations**
   - Oversee opening and closing tasks
   - Coordinate delivery to customers
   - Oversee housekeeping
   - Handle customer inquiries and complaints

4. **Reports**
   - Prepare monthly stock and sales report
   - Prepare a weekly report on the performance of the shop's activities and promotions

5. **Staff**
   - Help to orientate or guide new and junior staff
   - Assist in recruitment, selection, training, motivation and evaluation of junior staff

6. **Visual merchandising**
   - Ensure that merchandise is properly displayed
   - Follow up on visual merchandising of the shop

7. **Promotions**
   - Monitor and evaluate promotions in the shop

8. **Others**
   - Manage administrative work efficiently and effectively
   - Any other duties, which may be assigned by the Shop Manager from time to time

A Sample List of Terms and Conditions of Employment for a Supervisor

1. **Remuneration**

   Your salary will be S$1,500 per month with effect from 1 January 2008. You shall also receive a monthly commission of 1 percent of the shop's sales. Please note that your salary is confidential and you should not divulge or discuss it with anyone.

2. **Working hours**

   You will be required to work the hours necessary to complete your tasks but 44 hours per week should be the normal maximum. You will be entitled to three days off per fortnight. You shall not during the said term be engaged in any other employment or business outside the business of the company without the prior written consent of the company.

3. **Place of work**

   It is understood that you may be required to work from time to time in any of the branches of the company.

4. **Annual leave**

   Your annual leave entitlement will be 14 working days per year and cannot be accumulated or brought forward to another year unless approved by the company.

5. **Rules and regulations**

   You will be required to comply with all rules and regulations made by the company from time to time. A copy of the rules and regulations can be found in the staff handbook.

6. **Medical benefits and hospitalisation**

   You shall be entitled to free medical treatment of up to $500 per year by the company-appointed doctors. You shall be paid full normal pay during any absence caused by illness, up to a maximum of 30 days in any calendar year, if the doctor provides a medical certificate stating that you are not medically fit for normal duties. Staff shall enjoy hospitalization benefits according to the insurance policies purchased by the company. The types of benefits shall be extended in accordance to the staff's position in the company.

7. **Dental benefits**
   You shall be entitled to claim dental expenses of up to $50 per year.

8. **Staff purchase**
   You will be entitled to a staff discount of 20 percent on purchases made in the shop for yourself and/or for your immediate dependants only.

9. **Notice of termination**
   Written notice of termination shall be one month or pay in lieu of such notice from either party.

10. **Misconduct**
    In the event of misconduct or neglect of duty, the company reserves the right to terminate your service immediately.

11. **Disclosure of information**
    You shall not divulge directly or indirectly to anyone any confidential information which comes to your knowledge in the course of your employment with the company.

12. **Accuracy of information**
    The company reserves the right to terminate your service immediately if proven that you have given false information to gain employment with the company.

RETAIL OPERATIONS

Financial Control

Pre-planning is the essence of good financial management. The financial problems experienced by many retail companies highlight the need for a thorough understanding of the financial implications of retail decisions.

The major objectives of financial management are:

- To obtain funds for business uses
- To maintain and increase the invested capital
- To generate income

▬ Financing the Initial Operation

When planning to open a shop, you must consider the necessity of having sufficient funds (that is, start-up costs) for the following:

- Pay for professional advice if needed
- Pay for legal fees
- Pay rent in advance
- Pay renovation cost
- Purchase fixtures and equipment
- Buy merchandise for resale
- Purchase signs and display materials
- Install a telephone and other utilities
- Buy office supplies
- Promote the shops for opening (for example, advertising, sales promotion)
- Buy business insurance
- Pay for licence, permits and miscellaneous fees

To run a successful business, you must have working capital, that is, enough funds to permit the timely payment of required business expenses, from the day the business starts. The start of the business may have already depleted the majority of your cash resources. Thus you have to begin with enough cash to honour the terms of all investments, pay for expenses and still maintain an adequate cash balance.

To operate comfortably and without financial pressure, it is important to conduct a thorough research of all cost factors and standard operating ratios, and to prepare a financial worksheet to outline the start-up costs and the operating expenses for at least the first three months. Some operating expenses include the following:

- Owner's salary
- Salaries and commissions
- Rent
- Utilities
- Inventory
- Maintenance and supplies
- Repayment of loan
- Interest
- Accounts receivable
- Advertising and promotions
- Petty cash

▬ Budgetary Control

A budget is a plan that estimates future sales, expenses or some other financial aspects of a company over a specific period of one, three or six months. These estimates are based on past experience, present economic conditions and future plans. The actual figures are then compared with the estimates to determine how well specific areas are staying within the estimates. Many well-managed shops use budgets to plan, evaluate and control retail operations.

Generally, there are three main types of budgets that are interrelated:

1. The operating budget which consists of the sales budget, merchandise budget and the expense budget

2. The cash budget

3. The capital budget

The Sales Budget

One of the key items in the merchandise and cash budget is the sales forecast. This is true because

> an overestimation or underestimation of sales has a serious effect on merchandising decisions as well as cash flow.

A typical retailer develops forecasts on the basis of the following:

- Experience and knowledge of the field

- Input from suppliers and sales staff

- Past sales reports, paying special attention to factors such as comparability (for example, exceptional events that occurred in the previous year but not the current year) and environmental changes (for example, changes in consumers' taste of a product, recession and high unemployment)

The Merchandise Budget

Merchandise must be stocked to accommodate sales patterns. It is difficult to operate at a constant retail inventory level. Facing seasonal variations, you need to plan in advance to ensure a constant and adequate flow of merchandise to generate income.

The use of the stock-sales ratio can also help to estimate the amount of inventory needed to maintain that sales level. For example, if you estimate sales for the month to be S$20,000, and if you know from past experience that you need three times the sales volume to be in inventory, then you know that you will need S$60,000 in inventory to achieve the planned sales and still have sufficient opening inventory for the next month.

The Expense Budget

All the expenses (refer to the section on *Financing the Initial Operation* for examples of operating expenses) expected during the planning period, especially those that are incurred in generating the forecasted sales, should be included in this budget.

Expenses can be classified into fixed or variable expenses:

- Fixed expenses are those that do not vary with the volume of the business, such as insurance, property tax and depreciation.

- Variable expenses vary in direct proportion to the business volume, and they can therefore be controlled on a short-term basis. Such expenses include sales commissions, advertising, travel expenses and delivery expenses.

The Cash Budget

Continuous projection of an accurate cash flow (or a cash budget) will enable many small businesses to increase their operational performance and ensure sufficient funds for buying merchandise, paying for all operating expenses and for future growth. Such projection helps to predict when cash will come into the company and when payments of cash will have to be made, as well as the quantities coming in and going out.

Cash receipts are determined from forecasts of cash sales, accounts receivable collection and other sources of business income. Cash payments are based on anticipated operating expenses.

The Capital Budget

To ensure sufficient funds for future growth (for example, renovating the shop when needed, opening new outlets and replacement of or addition to existing assets), capital budgeting is necessary.

— Evaluation of Merchandise Effort

Merchandising efficiency is measured by:

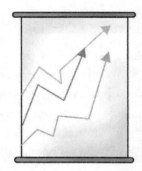

- Sales and markdowns
- Inventory and stock turnover
- Stock shortages
- Gross margin

Sales

Profit is the surplus after deducting the cost of goods sold and expenses from the sales revenue. However, greater sales do not necessarily lead to greater profit. Here are two examples:

1. If the economy is experiencing an inflation rate of 10 percent and your sales increase is only 5 percent, this indicates that the additional sales volume cannot keep pace with inflation.

2. If the sales record shows a 20 percent increase in dollar sales but a 15 percent decrease in units sold, this indicates that the merchandise is being sold at a higher price with fewer customers buying. If you have no intention to sell goods at a higher price at the expense of the number of units sold, you should analyse the cost and selling price of the merchandise carefully.

These examples show that you need to carefully analyse your sales figures to ensure that they are truly profit-producing.

Profit is essential for the survival of any business activity.

Markdowns

Generally, when sales figures are below those estimated, there will be excess merchandise. An effective way to speed up the sales of the merchandise or to dispose of merchandise that is unsaleable at its present price is to use markdowns.

An effective way to speed up the sales of merchandise is to use markdowns

Although markdowns eat into the profit, it is necessary to help the retailer get rid of outdated merchandise, create funds for purchasing new merchandise, foster customer goodwill or perhaps even to widen the base of potential customers.

> The ratio of old stock to new stock is an important standard for measuring your inventory's value and effectiveness.

It is important, however, to note that a shallow reduction is not an effective policy. Your first reduction should be the best one to ensure immediate sales increase.

Inventory

A major key to profitability is inventory control. It is important to know the amount of stock on hand at any point in time in order to make better merchandising decisions. Inventory control may be carried out periodically or on a continuous (perpetual) basis either in dollars or in units.

Periodic inventory is one method of keeping track of inventory by counting the stock on hand once, twice or more times per year on a specific date. However, this method is costly and can be time-consuming.

Perpetual inventory provides up-to-date information by monitoring merchandise movement into and out of the shop at any given time. Due to the cost and complexity, perpetual inventory control is better suited to high-ticket merchandise such as electrical appliances than to low-priced merchandise such as food. However, the use of POS equipment, as discussed in Chapter 15, can enhance such a method of inventory control.

For ease of planning, analysis and stocktaking, retailers generally maintain inventory records at retail prices and then convert the figure to its cost equivalent (where necessary).

Stock Turnover

Having too much inventory may lead to excessive markdowns if all the merchandise cannot be sold. It can also increase holding, storage and insurance costs. Having too little inventory may lead to lost sales because merchandise is not in stock when customers ask for the goods.

One way to measure whether there is too little or too much money invested in inventory is to calculate the number of times stock turns

The problem of overstocking

over in a given period. Stock turnover is a measure of how fast merchandise is sold and replaced. It indicates the number of times an average inventory is sold during the year.

A good turnover is a result of good merchandising management.

Stock turnover is also used to measure the retailer's ability to meet its cash obligations.

To derive the number of stock turns obtained in a given period, just divide the net sales of the period by the average inventory for that period. For example, if the net sales for the year is S$120,000 and the average inventory is S$20,000:

$$\text{Turnover rate} = \text{S\$120,000} \div \text{S\$20,000} = 6$$

This figure indicates that the average amount of merchandise on hand turns over (is sold) six times a year or once every two months (12 months ÷ 6).

Whether a stock turnover of six is good or bad depends on the type of retail business. In some retail businesses, such as supermarkets, turnover rates can be very high. This is because supermarket sales are more rapid and frequent replenishment is required. Thus supermarket retailers do not need to keep too much inventory on hand.

Others, such as apparel stores, may operate at very low turnover rates. This is because the system for manufacturing and distributing apparel requires retailers to order in bulk and therefore, it is necessary to carry backup stock and backup stock tends to slow down the rate of stock turnover. Shops that carry high-priced merchandise, such as jewellery, generally show low turnover rates too.

Retailers should compare their turnover rates for previous periods to detect the relative frequency of sales activity. A significant change in a rate may call for an analysis of sales and inventory operations.

A fast stock turnover ensures better use of capital and shop space, as well as reduces outdated merchandise and insurance costs. There are several ways to increase stock turnover:

- Carry minimum slow-moving merchandise or do not sell them at all

- Reduce the number of lines carried and concentrate on key merchandise

- Negotiate with suppliers to speed up deliveries of merchandise ordered

- Reduce prices

- Increase sales promotions

However, the above suggestions must be carried out with care as lowering prices may affect profitability, increasing promotions may increase expenses, and reducing inventory may lose customers and quantity discounts.

Stock Shortages

Stock shortage is the difference between the book value and the dollar value of a physical count. Stock shortages are unavoidable and will reduce gross margin. The retailer should attempt to minimise this loss of stock by recognising the reasons why they occur and by taking measures to prevent them. Shortages can be due to clerical errors, errors in selling, theft, errors in stock count or poor housekeeping.

Gross Margin

Gross margin or gross profit is the difference between net sales and the cost of goods sold. It is the initial level of profit (before deducting operating expenses) and must be sufficiently high to cover the operating expenses. Thus in making commitments to purchase merchandise, the retailer must always consider the mark-ups (or selling price) of the merchandise.

Both mark-ups and markdowns
have an immediate effect
on the gross margin.

Care must be taken in pricing merchandise for resale so that excessive markdowns can be avoided subsequently.

To improve the gross margin, the retailer can consider the following:

- Selling exclusive merchandise to enhance sales and discourage price comparison by customers
- Selling more of the higher-margin merchandise through advertising, better display and incentives to sales personnel
- Reducing frequent markdowns or discounts
- Reducing merchandise shortages

Evaluation of the Retail Performance

The basic tools of financial analysis are the balance sheet and the income statement of the company. These two statements summarise the company's activities in terms of financial impact.

Balance Sheet

A balance sheet contains a list of assets, liabilities and owner's equity. Assets and liabilities are further categorised as current or long-term. The balance sheet reflects the operating efficiency of the business by showing whether the company has over- or under-committed in asset holdings or is heavily in debt. Several measurements based on the balance sheet figures are useful to the retailer.

1. The current ratio indicates the retailer's ability to meet current debts with current assets.

   Current Ratio = Current Assets ÷ Current Liabilities

   For example, a ratio of 2:1 means that there is S$2 of current assets available to pay every S$1 of current liabilities. A current ratio of 2:1 is usually considered satisfactory.

2. The quick ratio measures the retailer's ability to meet current debts with assets that can be converted into cash immediately. This ratio is used instead of the current ratio when the inventory forms a large part of the current assets.

   Quick Ratio = (Cash + Receivables) ÷ Current Liabilities

   For example, a ratio of 1.5:1 means that there is S$1.50 of current assets available to pay every S$1 of current liabilities. A quick ratio of above 1 is usually considered favourable in securing loans from banks or financial institutions.

3. The debt-to-equity ratio measures the retailer's ability to meet all debts.

   Debt-to-Equity Ratio = Total Liabilities ÷ Owner's Equity

   The higher the ratio, the more difficult it is for the company to meet its debt. A ratio of below 1 is usually considered excellent.

Income Statement (Profit and Loss Statement)

An income statement consists of three sections:

1. Income from sales

2. Cost of goods sold

3. Operating expenses

The final amount at the end of the statement indicates whether the company has made a net profit or sustained a net loss over a specific period.

An example of an income statement is shown below. The income statement reflects the status of a company's health in terms of whether it is making sales, and equally important, whether it is making any profit on the sales. For example, it can reveal information such as a shop with a favourable gross margin but poor profits due to a lack of expense control.

EXAMPLE

The Shop
INCOME STATEMENT
Year Ending 31 December 2007

Gross sales		S$150,000
Less returns		S$ 20,000
Net sales		S$130,000
Less cost of goods sold		
Beginning inventory	S$30,000	
Purchases	S$50,000	
Total merchandise available for sale	S$80,000	
Less ending inventory	S$20,000	
Cost of goods sold		S$60,000
Gross margin		S$70,000
Operating expenses		
Salaries	S$30,000	
Rental	S$20,000	
Insurance	S$1,000	
Utilities	S$5,000	
Advertising	S$2,000	
Miscellaneous	S$2,000	
Total expenses		S$60,000
Net profit before tax		S$10,000

In the above example,

$$\text{Gross Margin on Sales} = \text{Gross Margin} \div \text{Net Sales}$$
$$= \text{S\$70,000} \div \text{S\$130,000}$$
$$= 54\%$$

This gross margin is very good. Gross margin on sales indicates the percentage of gross margin on every sales dollar. Typical gross margin rates in the retail industry can range from 20 percent to as much as 60 percent.

A careful analysis of the income statement shows that there are a few ways to improve a shop's profit performance.

- Increase sales but make sure that there is no proportionate increase in the cost of goods sold or operating expenses

- Decrease cost of goods sold but make sure that there is no proportionate decrease in sales or proportionate increase in operating expenses

- Decrease operating expenses but make sure that there is no proportionate decrease in sales or proportionate increase in cost of goods sold

As can be seen from above, a retailer may have to do more than simply increase sales to improve the retail performance.

> Retailers must analyse expenses in terms of their increases or decreases from one period to another frequently.

Percentages are a more realistic indication of such changes than the absolute dollar value. Operating expenses may also be evaluated as a percentage of sales. This practice allows retailers to judge the effect of operating expenses on sales volume.

Here is an example for evaluating the operating expenses (assuming net sales for The Shop is S$100,000 for 2008 and S$80,000 for 2007):

Operating expenses	2008		2007	
	S$	Percentage of net sales (%)	S$	Percentage of net sales (%)
Salaries	40,000	40	30,000	37.5
Rent	20,000	20	20,000	25.0
Utilities	11,000	11	8,000	10.0
Insurance	5,000	5	6,000	7.5
Advertising	5,000	5	6,000	7.5
Miscellaneous	5,000	5	3,000	3.7

Based on the above calculations, the retailer may ask the following questions:

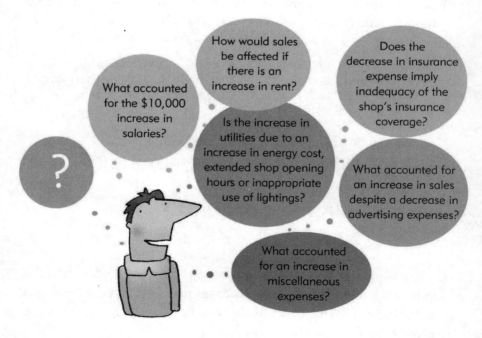

By answering the above questions, the retailer can better control or manage the operating expenses.

A combination of the balance sheet and the income statement amounts will also provide the retailer with other useful retail performance measures.

- The return on investment (ROI) indicates the percentage earned on investment in the business.

$$ROI = Net\ Income \div Owner's\ Equity$$

An ROI of 5 percent means that the retailer earned 5 percent on its investment in that year of calculation. Whether this figure is favourable or not depends on factors such as the outlook of the economy, the competitor's ROI or the possibility that the retailer may earn a higher return from other investments.

- Sales per square foot indicate how effectively sales are generated from the shop space devoted to selling.

$$Sales\ Per\ Square\ Foot = Net\ Sales \div Square\ Foot\ of\ Selling\ Space$$

A sales per square foot of S$100 means that every square foot of selling space is contributing S$100 to the shop's sales. The interpretation of this figure depends on factors such as past performance and the retail industry averages.

I need help...

How do I Increase my Profit?

The first responsibility of the owner is the survival of the business. It refers to not only the day-to-day survival, but also the long-term survival – three years, five years, ten years and so on. In an economy where consumer confidence is strong, the expectations for retail businesses will go up. Vendors expect higher sales at higher margins, landlords expect higher rents, employees expect higher wages, customers expect better prices and better service, and even your family expects better vacations!

However, given the realities of today's retailing scene where retailers face stiff competition, and watch margins slip while costs rise, relevant questions to ask are:

- The future of retailing: Are you up to it?

- Are you sharpening your competitive edge, for example, if your dealership disappears today, would any of your customers really care?

As the owner, you have to continually manage sales, margins, expenses, profits and people to ensure that they are aligned with your vision for the future.

In any retail business, some key business components to consider include the following:
- Market performance: Customer composition, profitability and market potential

- Product/category management: Sales, margin, inventory productivity
- Customer performance: Productivity and revenue opportunities
- Employee productivity: Processing sales, customer service
- Financial analysis: Ensure overheads are within estimates

Consider the situation in which a company identifies a problem:

- Sales and profits show a declining trend.
- Customer base is steadily ageing and visiting its outlets less frequently and spending less.
- Market is shrinking but competition is growing rapidly.

Clearly, the company must

- Reconsider its market positioning
- Attempt to increase its operating margins by consolidating outlets and merchandise assortment, and controlling operating cost
- Seek to participate in a more profitable market segment

As the owner of the shop, you are frequently challenged with the following:

- To increase sales revenue
- To increase gross profit
- To reduce operating costs
- To increase the productivity of assets

The table on the next two pages will elaborate on the tasks that a retailer can consider to achieve the above:

Objective	Means	Activities
1. Increase sales revenue	• Increase the number of purchasing customers	• Improve customer service, product quality and shop ambience
	• Increase the number of customer visits	• Monitor customer responses, buying behaviour and perception of your competitive offers
		• Add value to the customer offer (for example, add service to existing merchandise ranges such as installation services or disposal of replaced durables and so on)
	• Increase the size of customer purchase	• Offer coordinated merchandise ranges
		• Ensure merchandise availability
2. Increase gross profit	• Increase the average transaction	• Identify and promote impulse products with the core products
	• Improve the profitability of the merchandise range	• Identify gaps within the merchandise range (that is, whether you have missed out any related merchandise within a range)
		• Enhance customer movement within the shop through better shop layout
		• Display products with high profit margin prominently
	• Increase the merchandise margins	• Optimise the number of suppliers and negotiate for better support
		• Monitor the supplier's performance in terms of product sales, product availability, reliability, delivery terms of purchase and so on
		• Use bulk buying where possible
		• Review and monitor cost price versus selling price of all merchandise ranges

Objective	Means	Activities
3. Reduce operating costs	• Review and control all direct or indirect costs	• Review and monitor cost of goods sold and allowances given by suppliers • Review and monitor shop expenses • Review operating hours
4. Increase the productivity of assets	• Increase sales and contribution per square foot and per employee	• Review sales performance against forecasts and budget • Review return on stock investment • Review markdowns and losses • Review the space allocation and space utilisation by all merchandise • Monitor space performance • Monitor sales contribution per staff • Monitor selling costs

Index

RETAIL OPERATIONS

RETAIL OPERATIONS

SECOND EDITION

RETAIL OPERATIONS

Credits

Photograph credits

Chapter 1: p. 2 top left: ©iStockphoto.com/Jurga Rubinovaite; p. 2 top center: ©iStockphoto.com/Jacob Wackerhausen; p. 2 top right: © Ron Chapple Studios/Dreamstime.com; p. 2 center left: ©iStockphoto.com/Sean Locke; p. 2 center right: ©iStockphoto.com/Sean Locke; p. 2 bottom left: © Ron Chapple Studios/Dreamstime.com; p. 2 bottom right: ©iStockphoto.com/kutay tanir; p. 6: Kingsmen Creatives Ltd; p. 9 left: Robinsons Group of Stores; p. 9 right: Kingsmen Creatives Ltd; p. 18: Kingsmen Creatives Ltd; p. 20: © Fee Wan Ee/Dreamstime.com.

Chapter 2: p. 24 left: ©iStockphoto.com/Sean Locke; p. 24 center: ©iStockphoto.com/Don Bayley; p. 24 right: ©iStockphoto.com/Chris Schmidt; p. 43: ©iStockphoto.com/ Vinko Murko; p. 44: © Edyta Pawlowska/Dreamstime.com.

Chapter 3: p. 46 top left: © Olga Bogatyrenko/Dreamstime.com; p. 46 top right: Angie Tang; p. 46 bottom left: Angie Tang; p. 46 bottom right: Angie Tang; p. 48 top left: Angie Tang; p. 48 right: Angie Tang; p. 48 bottom left: Angie Tang; p. 52: Angie Tang; p. 54 top: ©iStockphoto.com/Imre Cikajlo; p. 54 bottom: Angie Tang; p. 55: Sarah Lim; p. 56: Angie Tang; p. 58 top: Angie Tang; p. 58 bottom: Kingsmen Creatives Ltd; p. 59: Angie Tang; p. 67: Angie Tang; p. 68: ©iStockphoto.com/Kheng Guan Toh; p. 69: Angie Tang; p. 70: Angie Tang.

Chapter 4: p. 72: © Chad Mcdermott/Dreamstime.com; p. 74: Robinsons Group of Stores; p. 79: Integrated Retail Management Consulting Pte Ltd; p. 80: Aussino Group Ltd.

Chapter 5: p. 84: Kingsmen Creatives Ltd; p. 88: © Tomasz Trojanowski/Dreamstime.com; p. 89: ©iStockphoto.com/Sean Locke; p. 96: Robinsons Group of Stores; p. 104: © Aliaksandr Zharnasek/Dreamstime.com; p. 108: Angie Tang.

Chapter 6: p. 114 top left: © Christy Thompson/Dreamstime.com; p. 114 center: ©iStockphoto.com/Sean Locke; p. 114 center right: ©iStockphoto.com/Igor Zhorov; p. 114 bottom left: © Olgalis/Dreamstime.com; p. 114 bottom right: ©iStockphoto.com/Sean Locke; p. 116: The Executive Home Store – XZQT; p. 119: © Scott Rothstein/Dreamstime.com.

Chapter 7: p. 130: Kingsmen Creatives Ltd; p. 134 top: Aussino Group Ltd; p. 134 bottom: Kingsmen Creatives Ltd; p. 138 top: Kingsmen Creatives Ltd; p. 138 center: Kingsmen Creatives Ltd; p. 138 bottom: Kingsmen Creatives Ltd; p. 139 top: Kingsmen Creatives Ltd; p. 139 bottom: Kingsmen Creatives Ltd; p. 140: Aussino Group Ltd; p. 146: © Zts/Dreamstime.com.

Chapter 8: p. 152: ©Sebastian Kaulitzki/Dreamstime.com; p. 155: Agnes Lim; p. 156: © Raycan/Dreamstime.com; p. 157 top: © Jonas Marcos San Luis/Dreamstime.com; p. 157 bottom: © Stephen Finn/Dreamstime.com; p. 158: © Qilux/Dreamstime.com; p. 159: Sarah Lim; p. 163 top left: © Ti_to_tito/Dreamstime.com; p. 163 top right: Integrated Retail Management Consulting Pte Ltd; p. 163 bottom: Kingsmen Creatives Ltd; p. 169: © Teresa Azevedo/Dreamstime.com; p. 170: Robinsons Group of Stores.

Chapter 9: p. 172: © Alex Brosa/Dreamstime.com; p. 174: © Scott Rothstein/Dreamstime.com.

Chapter 10: p. 182: Kingsmen Creatives Ltd; p. 186: Kingsmen Creatives Ltd; p. 187: Kingsmen Creatives Ltd; p. 189: The Executive Home Store – XZQT; p. 192: © Fee Wan Ee/Dreamstime.com.

Chapter 11: p. 196: © Geoffrey Whiting/Dreamstime.com.

Chapter 12: p. 234: Kingsmen Creatives Ltd; p. 237: Aussino Group Ltd; p. 238: Angie Tang; p. 240: Ricky Lim; p. 241: Ricky Lim.

Chapter 13: p. 252 top: © Suprijono Suharjoto/Dreamstime.com; p. 252 bottom: © Dmitry Kosterev/Dreamstime.com; p. 254 top: Kingsmen Creatives Ltd; p. 254 bottom: Kingsmen Creatives Ltd; p. 255 top: Angie Tang; p. 255 bottom: Angie Tang; p. 256 left: Robinsons Group of Stores; p. 256 right: Robinsons Group of Stores; p. 257 top: Aussino Group Ltd; p. 257 bottom: Angie Tang; p. 259: Robinsons Group of Stores; p. 260: Aussino Group Ltd; p. 261: Aussino Group Ltd; p. 262: Robinsons Group of Stores; p. 263 top: Robinsons Group of Stores; p. 263 bottom left: Robinsons Group of Stores; p. 263 bottom right: Robinsons Group of Stores; p. 264: Angie Tang; p. 265 top left: Kingsmen Creatives Ltd; p. 265 top right: Aussino Group Ltd; p. 265 bottom: © Johnny Lye/Dreamstime.com.